HEIDEGGER AND DEATH

A CRITICAL EVALUATION

MONIST MONOGRAPH
Number 1

HEIDEGGER ON DEATH: A CRITICAL EVALUATION

Paul Edwards

Editor: Eugene Freeman

Managing Editor: Sherwood J.B. Sugden

THE HEGELER INSTITUTE
publishers of
THE MONIST
An International Quarterly Journal
of General Philosophical Inquiry
Box 600, La Salle, Illinois 61301

To order books from Open Court, call
toll-free 1-800-815-2280 or visit our website
at www.opencourtbooks.com.

This book has been reproduced in a print-on-demand
format from the 1979 Hegeler Institute printing. This work
originally appeared as "Monist Monograph Number 1."

Open Court Publishing Company is a division
of Carus Publishing Company.

To the Memory of

BERTRAND RUSSELL

enemy of humbug and mystification

"As men abound in copiousness of language, so they become more wise or more mad than ordinary."

—Thomas Hobbes

"Act as if you were going to live forever and cast your plans way ahead. By this I mean that you must feel responsible without time limitation, and the consideration whether you may or may not be around to see the results should never enter your thoughts."

—Walter Gropius

CONTENTS

PREFACE

Philosophers who reject Heidegger's theories have generally preferred to ignore them. As a result practically no detailed critical examinations of his work exist. This is doubly unfortunate. It is impossible to refer students and other inquirers to an authoritative treatment of Heidegger's philosophy. It also leaves the few good ideas that are found in Heidegger's work shrouded in the obscure and barbarous jargon of his writings and those of his followers. The present monograph is intended to do something toward filling the gap just mentioned.

I have examined in detail all except two of Heidegger's theses about death. Among those which I have discussed very fully are the three that have received the widest acclaim—that human life is "being-towards-death," that death is "untransferable," and that it is "the possibility of the impossibility of existing." On behalf of the last of these, in particular, grandiose claims have been made. It has been asserted, both by Heidegger himself and by several of his followers, that Heidegger has here "unveiled" the true meaning of death. Because of space limitations I have not discussed the so-called "wholeness" problem. I have also not undertaken an analysis of the slippery concept of "authenticity" and I have not attempted an evaluation of the contention by various Heideggerians that enormous benefits would accrue to the human race if people started thinking about death "authentically" in Heidegger's sense of this word. Furthermore, I have confined myself to what Heidegger has to say about death in *Being and Time*. There are occasional brief references to death in several of the later writings, but nothing that amounts to a discussable thesis. However, an exhaustive treatment would also cover the later works. I intend to rectify these omissions in my book *A Critical Examination of Martin Heidegger's Philosophy* which will be published by the Free Press of New York. This book will also contain detailed discussions of other major topics in Heidegger's philosophy, especially Being and "the Nothing." About "the Nothing" I have said a good deal in the last section of the present study, but for the most part only in so far as it relates to anxiety and death.

Earlier versions of several sections appeared in *Mind* (1975) and *The Monist* (1976). I am grateful to the editors of these journals for allowing me to reprint material which appeared in these articles. I wish to thank my friends Donald Levy and Michael Wreen for reading the manuscript and making valuable suggestions. I would also like to thank my friend Seymour Schuman who was extremely helpful during a long period of illness and partial incapacitation when I was unable to work in libraries. Because of his aid the sources needed for work on the present as well as other projects were available to me.

Friends who are familiar with the tediousness of most of the Heideggerian literature have asked me how I have the patience to go through "all this stuff." The answer is that there are often special rewards. Some topics, especially time and death, set these writers aflame and unleash unsuspected talents. However gloomy the subject of death may be, a study of certain Heideggerian "quests" and arguments concerning death is not gloomy at all but on the contrary pure joy. As philosophers these writers may be a failure, but as providers of mirth they are a huge success. I have made it a point to share some of the juciest pickings with my readers.

—Paul Edwards
New York City
December, 1979.

HEIDEGGER AND DEATH: A CRITICAL EVALUATION

Writing in an article in celebration of Heidegger's seventieth birthday, the Japanese philosopher, Hajime Tanabe, speaks of Heidegger's philosophy as a "unique and towering monument" with which the achievements of other "contemporaries cannot even be compared." Tanabe observes with evident delight that Heidegger's influence is "no longer confined to Europe but reaches even as far as Japan" and not only to Japan, but to the whole world. Heidegger's disciples, we are told, "are now active everywhere in the world." What "deeply moved" Tanabe in his first contact with Heidegger was the fact that "in his thinking concern with death became the center of philosophy as well as its support."[1] Similar expressions of admiration for Heidegger's discussions of death are found in the writings of many of his disciples. Thus, William Barrett, in the course of much other praise of Heidegger, asserts that "his analysis of death is perhaps the most important and satisfying interpretation in his whole picture of man."[2] Father James M. Demske, who has been deeply impressed by "the originality of Heidegger's conception" tells us that Heidegger "not only poses the problem [of death] with a previously unheard-of force and sharpness," but also "confers upon it a new ontological depth."[3] John Wild, who does not wholly approve of Heidegger's later philosophy, remarks that *Being and Time* has "shed much needed light" on death, and that Heidegger's treatment of the subject is "packed with suggestive interpretations."[4]

In the present study I wish to explain some of the reasons why I do not regard Heidegger's "analysis" of death as a "satisfying interpretation" and why I do not find in his discussions of the subject a "previously unheard-of force and sharpness." I shall examine several of Heidegger's main theses in some detail. Such a critical examination will show that the praise lavished on Heidegger's teachings about death by his adulators is not justified.

1. The Alleged Loneliness of Death

The first Heideggerian doctrine I wish to consider is usually expressed by the statement that all human beings die alone. Heidegger himself never uses "allein" which is the German word for "alone," but he uses various expressions which come to the same thing. He constantly speaks of death as a "non-relational possibility." When death "is the issue," he writes, "all Being-alongside the things with which we concern ourselves, and all Being-with Others, will fail us."[5] When Dasein (a human being) stands before its death, i.e., when he is face to face with "the possibility of no-longer-being-able-to-be-there," then "all its relations to any other Dasein have been undone" (BT, p.294). "The non-relational character of death, as understood in anticipation, individualizes Dasein down to itself" (BT, p. 308). In this "distinct possibility of its own self," a possibility "in which its very Being is the issue," Dasein "has been wrenched away from the 'they' [other people]" (BT, p. 307). Death "must be taken over by Dasein alone."[6]

Heideggerians writing in English have used words like "alone" and "isolated" to express this doctrine; and in doing so, they have, I think, been quite faithful to Heidegger's intentions. Death, according to John Macquarrie, "isolates the individual. He must die himself alone."[7] "This thing at least," writes John Wild, speaking of death, "I must do alone"[8] and a little later he remarks that death "is an actual act lived through by an individual alone."[9] "Everyone," in the words of Calvin O. Schrag, "must die alone."[10] "The more resolutely we advance toward" death, in the words of Father Demske, "the more clearly we see the aspects of aloneness which characterize Dasein in its being-unto-death. Advancing reveals that all being-with the other beings . . . fades away in the sight of death."[11] "Each of us," writes Father Ladislaus Boros, a Hungarian admirer of Heidegger, "must accept death absolutely alone."[12] Heidegger's analysis of "Dasein's existentiality," according to Michael Gelven, the author of a rhapsody entitled *A Commentary on Heidegger's "Being and Time"*, "shows us that . . . I alone will die my death." Furthermore, "when my consciousness becomes aware of death, it projects before me that I am really going to die, and that when I do I will die alone."[13] Death, to quote J. Glenn Gray, one of the first of Heidegger's champions in the United States and co-editor of the English-language edition of Heidegger's works, "is unshareable, the most isolated, separate of life's possibilities, and for that reason the most significant."[14] To this Gray adds, speaking no doubt from extensive personal experience, "I always die alone."[15] Father William J. Richardson, the author of an enormously detailed study of all phases of Heidegger's philosophy which is widely regarded as the standard commentary on the subject, wholeheartedly accepts Heidegger's view about the inevitable aloneness of the dying individual. A human being "dies . . . by its self [sic] stripped of all relationship to others, isolated completely."[16] There is apparently something superficially very plausible about the contention that everybody must die alone. For it is endorsed by philosophers who are critical of Heidegger in other contexts and it is also asserted, as if it were something self-evident, by people who probably never heard of Heidegger. Thus Marjorie Grene, in an otherwise highly critical study of Heidegger, is full of praise of him on this particular issue, remarking: "It is in the face of death that each man stands most strikingly and irrevocably alone."[17] Similarly, Leonard Bernstein observed a few years ago, in a funeral oration for the distinguished mezzo-soprano, Jennie Tourel, that "she knew that birth and death are lonely acts, painfully private and incapable of being shared."[18]

The question we shall ask about this doctrine is not simply "is it true?" For, any statement can be made true by suitable definitions. The question we have to ask is whether the doctrine is true in a sense in which it would constitute a discovery or a significant insight. Before we try to answer this question it should be emphasized that Heidegger and his followers are offering us a proposition which is universal and, in some important sense, necessary. They are not merely asserting, what nobody would dispute, that some or many human beings die alone. They assert that this is true of all human beings in all ages and that it is necessarily true of all human beings simply as a consequence of their mortality.

I will begin my critical observations by pointing out that the statement "all human beings die alone" can be understood in three reasonably straightforward senses and that in each of these it is quite certainly false. In a very obvious sense a person dies alone if no other human being is with him when he dies. A man driving by himself, who has a fatal heart attack, would be dying alone in this sense. A few years ago, Bishop James Pike, and his wife, got lost in the desert in Israel. The Bishop stayed with the jeep that had broken down while his wife went for help. He died before the rescuers arrived. He too died alone in the sense under discussion. In this sense many people die alone and many do not.

There is another sense in which it would be natural to speak of somebody as dying alone or in isolation, even if other human beings are physically with him during his last moments. In this sense a person is dying alone if he is psychologically isolated, i.e., if there are no other human beings near him with whom he has any strong emotional bonds. Elisabeth Kübler-Ross and other psychologists have movingly described the sufferings of dying patients who, in addition to their physical torment, suffer extreme loneliness as a result of the coldness of nurses and doctors and the inability of relatives to be open and honest. It is important to emphasize that, while a great many people do die alone in the second sense, not all do; and it is certainly not necessary, either in the sense of logical or in the sense of factual necessity, that human beings should do so.

That it is not at all necessary is illustrated in Gerhardt Hauptmann's play, *Vor Sonnenuntergang*, which deals with the last year in the life of Matthias Clausen, an elderly and extremely wealthy industrialist. Clausen is a widower with two married daughters from whom he is estranged and he feels totally alone. He plans to kill himself but is talked out of suicide by a lovely young typist. They fall in love. He proposes marriage, but she refuses since it might be thought that she was marrying him for his money. They live together and eventually do get married. His daughters and their husbands institute proceedings to have Matthias declared mentally incompetent. He fights back and suffers a heart attack. As he is dying he tells his grief-stricken young wife that there is nothing to regret. "The last year, since I have known you, is the only time I really lived—the only time that I was close to another human being." Matthias Clausen did *not* die alone in the emotional or psychological sense; and surely the same has been true of *some* human beings in real life. David Hume, to give just one famous example, was never more contented than during the last six months of his life when he knew that he was dying. He never felt closer to his friends than during this period and he continued to take an active interest in the world around him, including the latest publications in various fields. "Were I to name a period of my life which I should most choose to pass over again," he wrote in his short autobiography while he was dying, "I might be tempted to point to this later period."[19]

There is a further sense in which people are sometimes said to die alone, where "dying alone" is opposed to "dying together" rather than to "dying not alone." In *The Savage God*, A. Alvarez tells the story of Jacques Vaché, a bizarre young poet, who had a decisive influence on André Breton, the founder of surrealism. Vaché was convinced of the utter futility of life and adopted as his guiding principle what he called "umore"—a malignant and self-destructive irony. He was conscripted into the French army during the First World War. In a letter from the front he explained that he objected to being killed in the war, adding

> I shall die when I want to die, and then I shall die with somebody else. To die alone is boring, I should prefer to die with one of my best friends.[20]

In 1919, when the war was over, Vaché died in accordance with these specifications. He invited two friends to take an opium "trip" with him. He administered a lethal dose to his unsuspecting friends and an equally lethal dose to himself. He thus did not die alone.[21]

It should be pointed out in passing that Vaché was using the expression "dying alone" in a confusing and improper way. If his two friends had been saved, it would have been correct to say that he, alone of the three, died and not that he died alone. "Alone" is here equivalent to "only" and it qualifies "he" and not "dying." However, let us waive this point and accept Vaché's way of talking as a third sense in which one may speak of human beings as dying alone. Clearly, as in the case of the other two senses, some human beings die alone in this sense and some do not. If only one of a dozen hostages is executed, he died alone. If all or several of them are executed at the same time, they did not die alone. As before, the assertion that all human beings die alone is seen to be false.

It should be noted that the Heideggerians do not base their statement "All men die alone" on detailed inspections of the last moments of human beings. As *they* use the expression "dying alone" we can *deduce* that a person died alone from the mere fact that he died. No inquiry whatever is needed into the circumstances of his death. If he died, surrounded by other human beings to whom he had deep emotional ties, he nevertheless died alone simply because he died. This gives us a clue as to what has happened here. "Dying alone" has been redefined so as to be logically equivalent to "dying." As the Heideggerians use "alone" (or rather as it must be interpreted if their statement is not to be plainly false), it is *logically* impossible for a person to die and not to die alone. If "alone" had some additional content, it would be possible to describe what it would be like for a person to die without dying alone; but, as the Heideggerians use these words, such a description is not possible. The way in which they write suggests that the logical relation between "dying" and "dying alone" is like the relation between "dying" and "dying in poverty" or "dying" and "dying in bed." In both these cases we clearly have a synthetic relation: "dying in poverty" means more than "dying" and the same is true of "dying in bed." The same is also true of "dying alone" in any of the three senses mentioned earlier, but it is not true of "dying alone" as the Heideggerians must use this expression if their statement that everybody dies alone is not to be false. As they are committed to using these words, the relation between "dying" and "dying alone" is like the relation between "father" and "parent." The upshot of our discussion is that if the Heideggerian statement is interpreted in such a way that it says something interesting, then it is clearly false; and if it is interpreted so as to make it true, it becomes nothing more than a rhetorical way of asserting the exceedingly familiar fact that everybody dies some day. The triviality of the Heideggerian doctrine is not at once apparent to everybody only because, in any of its familiar senses, "dying alone" *does* mean more than "dying" and because the reader has not been warned (and the Heideggerians themselves have probably not realized) that "alone" has been redefined.

The emptiness of the Heideggerian doctrine, what may not unfairly be described as its bogus character, becomes particularly clear when one reflects that it *seems* to, but does not in fact, have any practical implications. Let us suppose that a "believer" in this "theory" has a wife and children to whom he is attached in much the same way as non-Heideggerians have been attached to their wives and children. Let us suppose that he has an accident and is taken to a hospital. He has reason to believe that he may die very shortly. If the word "alone" were used in any of its familiar senses in the Heideggerian statement "all human beings die alone" and if the statement were true, then our Heideggerian should *not* send for his family. This would be entirely pointless since all human beings die alone. In practice he would send for his wife and children just like any other reasonably normal human being. In other words, acceptance of the doctrine is entirely compatible with all the usual distinctions between dying alone and not dying alone; and our Heideggerian, if he has normal human impulses, will not want to be alone but with those he loves.

Some readers are likely to object to the above criticisms that, although not everybody may be *dying* alone, it is nevertheless true, and necessarily true, that *in death* everybody is alone. These are the very words used by the translators of *Sein und Zeit* in an explanatory footnote in which they assert and apparently regard it as self-evident that "in death Dasein is cut off from relations with others" (BT, p. 294n.). Such a rejoinder will seem plausible to all who are under the influence of the picture of death as a kind of sleep or rest. Proust somewhere speaks of "the mind's inability, when it ponders death, to picture something other than life" and I think it is true that, while part of the time we know perfectly well that the dead are not sleeping or resting (i.e., alive, but in a very passive sort of way), at other times we do think of them as sleeping in the grave or as somehow continuing to exist in a dark abode.[22] If a dead person were indeed sleeping in his grave, he would presumably be alone, both because nobody else is in the coffin with him, and, more fundamentally, because unlike the living, he would be incapable of communicating with anybody. A little sober reflection will show that this rejoinder is absurd. The dead are not resting or sleeping. Sleep and rest are states of *living* organisms. The statement that somebody is alone presupposes that he is alive; and while it is intelligible, though it may not be true to say about a *dying* person that he is alone, it is nonsense to say that a dead man is alone.

2. The Untransferability of Death

Death is not only Dasein's nonrelational possibility. It is also its "ownmost possibility." "With death," writes Heidegger, "Dasein stands before itself in its ownmost potentiality-for-being" (BT, p. 294). This ownmost and nonrelational possibility "is at the same time the uttermost one" (*ibid.*). "Ownmost" is the word M-R use to translate the German "eigenst" which literally means "most my own." If we adopt a completely literal translation, Heidegger is asserting that my death is more mine than anything else; and it is not surprising to find Father Demske telling us that death is "the most intimate . . . possibility of one's own existence"[23] and Glen Gray speaking of death as "this most private . . . possibility"[24] and "the most intimate experience of all."[25]

At first sight this sounds like mere gibberish. In one sense death is not "mine" at all. As we shall see in detail in the next section, Heidegger and his disciples constantly confuse death with our thoughts and emotions about death. My thoughts and emotions about death are indeed "mine," but it is difficult to see why they should be regarded as "more mine" than for example my desire to love and be loved or my desire to enjoy life. Heidegger appears to be under the spell of some kind of nebulous picture which he is also trying to foist on his readers—a picture of death concealed deep inside every one of us. However, this is not all he is doing. The statement that death is our ownmost possibility appears to be a summary of something he had defended with some feeling earlier in the same chapter, namely, that, as his followers have frequently put it, death is "untransferable." About ten pages before first using the word "ownmost," Heidegger refers to those "possibilities" in which one Dasein *can* represent another:

> Indisputably, the fact that one Dasein can be *represented* by another belongs to its possibilities of Being in Being-with-one-another in the world. In everyday concern, constant and manifold use is made of such representability. Whenever we go anywhere or have anything to contribute, we can be represented by someone within the range of that "environment" with which we are most closely concerned.
>
> Representability is not only quite possible but is even constitutive for our being with one another. *Here* one Dasein can and must, within certain limits, "*be*" another Dasein. (BT, pp. 283–84, Heidegger's italics)

In the case of death, on the other hand, no such substituting or representing is possible:

> However, this possibility of representing breaks down completely if the issue is one of representing that possibility-of-Being which makes up Dasein's coming to an end. (BT, p. 284)

Again:

> Dying . . . is essentially mine in such a way that no one can be my representative. (BT, p. 297)

> Death *is* always one's own. (BT, p. 309, G. 265, Heidegger's italics)[26]

Disciples from different parts of the world have enthusiastically endorsed these remarks. Hinrich Knittermeyer, the author of one of the first historical surveys of existentialism, is emphatic that in death a human being cannot be "replaced." Nobody, he goes on, can "absolve somebody else from dying. . . . Death occurs only in the singular."[27] Johannes Pfeiffer, another German admirer, assures us that "anxiety in the face of death, so far from degrading a human being, liberates him and brings him his true dignity. . . . For death is always his own; in relation to his death no individual human being can be represented by another."[28] J. L. Mehta, an Indian devotee who has had "the privilege of meeting and talking with Professor Heidegger more than once in his own house," and whose stupendous aggregation of paraphrases, *The Philosophy of Martin Heidegger*, has been hailed by other Heideggerians as "one of the finest books to appear on Heidegger in any language," is in total agreement. "No deputizing," he writes, "is possible when it comes to that possibility of being which consists of the coming-to-an-end of Dasein and which endows it with its wholeness."[29] None of Heidegger's American supporters voice any dissent on this topic. Death, according to John Wild, "is not a replaceable, interchangeable function."[30] Death, in the words of Glenn Gray, "is unshareable . . . it is always and ever my own . . . no one can take my place in death, nor can I, in this sense, ever die for another."[31] "Death," writes Schrag, "is indelibly my own and therefore non-transferable . . . No substitution of roles is possible when it comes to dying."[32] "If there is anything that is my own," Gelven exclaims, "it is my death . . . every man dies his own death. It cannot be shared or be taken over by someone else."[33] "Though another may die in my place," writes William H. Bossart, "another can never die my death."[34] "My death," to quote William Barrett, "is essentially mine."[35]

It is important to point out that, in one fairly obvious sense, it is not true that one cannot, ever or in principle, get somebody else to die in one's place. In Schiller's poem "Die Bürgschaft" ("The Bond") the tyrant, Dionys, sentences Möros to death by crucifixion for attempting to assasinate him. Möros begs for three days' grace to get his sister married off. Dionys agrees on condition that Möros's best friend remain behind as hostage. If Möros does not return in time the friend is to die in his place. An interesting actual case of this kind involving Thomas Paine occurred during the French Revolution. Paine was at that time an exile from England where the government had ordered a warrant for his arrest and also instigated an unbelievably vicious campaign of slander and vilification. Although he was himself later condemned to death, in the earlier stages of the Revolution Paine was a deputy in the Constituent Assembly and exercised considerable influence. An Englishman by the name of Zachariah Wilkes had been condemned for another's offense. Wilkes appealed to Paine for help, although, as he put it, "Paine must hate and detest the name of any Englishman—pelted, insulted, persecuted and slandered" as he had been by the English government. Paine had Wilkes released and stood as hostage in his place while Wilkes went to England. Paine's confidence was not abused. Wilkes returned in time with proof of his innocence. In these cases the hostages did not in fact die in the place of the people they represented, but they easily might have done so. In principle a substitution of this kind is entirely possible and there is no doubt that, in the sense just explained, people have on occasion died in the place of other human beings.

Heidegger is aware of these facts, but he dismisses them as irrelevant to his point:

No one can take the Other's dying away from him. Of course someone can "go to his death for another." But that always means to sacrifice oneself for the Other *"in some definite affair."* Such "dying for" can never signify that the Other has thus been delivered from his death in even the slightest degree. Dying is something that every Dasein itself must take upon itself at the time. By its very essence, death is in every case mine, in so far as it "is" at all. (BT, p. 286, G p. 240; Heidegger's italics)

It is evident that Heidegger ends up with two statements which are not affected by the occurrence or the possibility of the kind of substitution we discussed in the last paragraph. They are, first, the statement that nobody can die another's death, i.e., that the death a person dies is his and not somebody else's, and, second, the statement that although one person can sacrifice himself for another, he cannot *ultimately* deliver him from his death, i.e., prevent him from dying.

It seems to me that both of these statements are true, but that both of them are trite, though for different reasons. The first is what we may call a "grammatical" truth. It in effect simply states a rule of language. It tells us that if there are two human beings, or for that matter two animals or living beings of any kind, A and B, then if A dies it is incorrect to say that A dies B's death and vice versa. The statement that nobody can die another's death appears to assert a certain fact, a certain limitation or incapacity of human beings. In this it seems to be like the statement that no human being can run a hundred yards in less than five seconds or that no human being can indefinitely resist the kind of torture to which the defendants in the notorious Trotzky-trials were subjected in the Soviet Union in the 1930's. The latter statements are true, if they are true, because of certain facts. Heidegger's statement similarly seems to assert the existence of certain physical or psychological limitations. In fact, however, it does nothing of the kind. The reason why I cannot die somebody else's death has nothing to do with physical or psychological limitations. It is the same as the reason why if I have gout, it must be my own gout and not somebody else's or why if I have a cramp in my right foot, the cramp must be mine and not the cramp of Richard Nixon or of Frank Sinatra or of any other human being. To say that I have a cramp in my foot includes as part of what I am asserting that the cramp is mine. This is not an extra fact, over and above the fact that I have a cramp. Exactly the same applies to the statement that I will die. It includes as part of its content that the death I will die is mine. The explicit statement of a rule of language is not necessarily trite. It may be important and illuminating if it is a rule that is not always obeyed and if violation of the rule leads to confused theorizing. However, in the present case there is no reason to believe that anybody has ever had the slightest tendency to go against the rule in question. When President Kennedy died, it did not occur to anybody, including the most inauthentic nonexistentialist, to say that President Kennedy died the death of Richard Nixon or the death of Barry Goldwater or the death of anybody other than his own. It is clear that when William Barrett said that his death was "essentially" his, he erred on the side of moderation. Our linguistic rules guarantee that when Barrett dies, his death will be his, not just "essentially", but utterly, totally, and without qualification.

The statement that ultimately nobody can deliver somebody else from dying is also trite, but for a different reason. It is a factual statement and not the formulation of a rule of language, but in effect it asserts nothing more than that ultimately everybody dies. It is important to insert here the word "ultimately" because, nonultimately, other people may "deliver" me from my death, in the way explained earlier. *Ultimately* they cannot deliver me from my death, but this is so because ultimately I am going to die. Heidegger's statement does not assert any fact over and above the fact that I am going to die: it simply reasserts this fact and hence it is not a discovery or an insight or a contribution to our understanding of anything.

There is a relatively easy explanation of why Heidegger's untransferability doctrine *seems* to amount to more than the two trite statements just discussed. It seems to come to more because, after admitting that the initial claim of untransferability is false in the sense in which it is most naturally construed, Heidegger nevertheless retains the original language. Let us distinguish between the following three statements:

(1) In the matter of death no human being can substitute for another.
(2) The death a person dies is and must be his own.
(3) Nobody can ultimately deliver another human being from dying.

Unlike (2) and (3), (1), as it is most naturally understood, is not trite. It makes a most interesting claim—the claim that, unlike in such matters as lecturing or singing an operatic role or treating a patient or defending a client in a criminal case, representation or substitution is not possible when it comes to dying. In practice this would mean that a lecturer can, at least in principle, get somebody else to take his place, that singers, doctors, lawyers can get substitutes for their respective professional jobs, but that it is *in principle* impossible to get somebody else to die in one's place. This claim, if true, would be most interesting; but we have seen that it is not true. Heidegger acknowledges this and shifts to (2) and (3). However, he retains the initial language, suggesting quite falsely that (1) has been vindicated.

It will be worth while to show in some detail, that, as far as "representability" or "substitutability" is concerned, there is a strict parallel between dying on the one hand and such activities as lecturing, performing in an opera, treating patients, or defending a client, on the other. For this purpose I will imagine a strange and perverted land, called "Clockwork Orange," in which there is a society of psychotic sadists known as "the Torturers." This society has been granted a special charter by the government allowing them to put to death one person at their meeting on the first Monday evening of every month. The one condition is that the individual they decide to kill must never have offended any member of that society. Once they pick their victim, the police is instructed to deliver him alive. Let us suppose that I have been picked for next Monday and the government has issued a warrant for my arrest. The Torturers decided that this time they wanted a professional philosopher and they randomly selected me from a list of members of the Philosophical Association of Clockwork Orange. Let us furthermore suppose that I have a devoted assistant, also a professional philosopher, by the name of Samuel Blau, who has often substituted for me in my classes at the leading adult education school in Clockwork Orange, the New School for Humanistic Studies. I don't particularly want to die next Monday, not because I have anything against death, but because I am in the middle of an article on Heidegger which I don't want to leave unfinsihed. I therefore ask Samuel Blau if he would be so kind as to substitute for me and he readily agrees. I call the secretary of the Torturers who does not object so long as Blau is also a professional philosopher which I assure him he is. Finally, the chief of police agrees to the substitution. Blau is thereupon apprehended and killed at the Monday meeting. Now, I wish to insist that Blau's substitution for me in the matter of dying is, in all relevant respects, *exactly* parallel to his substituting for me at the New School for Humanistic Studies. He substituted at the New School by lecturing and discussing the topic that I would have discussed if I had gone in. He produced certain effects upon the students analogous to those I would have produced. He substitutes for me at the Monday meeting of the Tortuters by doing or suffering what I would have done or suffered and he produces effects on the audience (presumably of sadistic delight) analogous to those which my dying would have produced. If somebody now says "but he would die his death and not yours," this is true but irrelevant—irrelevant to the fact of his substituting for me. He also did not give my lecture; or, assuming that I had written it out and he merely read it, his reading of the lecture was *his* and not mine. If somebody then maintains "but his appearing at the Monday meeting of the Torturers does not prevent you from eventually dying," the answer is again that this is true but irrelevant. It has nothing whatever to do with the fact of his substituting for me on that occasion. It is no more relevant than if somebody had said "Sam Blau did not really substitute for you at the New School last Tuesday because although he showed up and gave a most interesting lecture on the topic you were supposed to cover he will not substitute for you in all your future classes." But, it will be said, ultimately neither Blau nor anybody else can prevent me from dying, while in principle somebody else can substitute for all the lectures I will ever be scheduled to give. This is true, but once more irrelevant. It shows that Heidegger's proposition (3) is true. It does not show that Blau did not represent me at the meeting of the Torturers in *exactly* the same sense in which he represented me at the New School; and more generally it does not show in the slightest that death is untransferable in the only natural sense of the word.

Just like Heidegger's procedure, this retort involves a shift from the interesting but false assertion (1) to the true but platitudinous statement (3).

The upshot of our discussion is that the untransferability-doctrine is true in senses in which it is trite, and false in the sense in which it would be interesting. It seems both interesting and true only if the shift which I have been describing is not clearly noticed.

3. Being-Towards-Death

All major existentialists who have written about death (with the one notable exception of Sartre) oppose their own teaching on the subject to what they refer as the "external" view of death. This is a view shared by the pagan philosophers of antiquity, by Hegel and his disciples, by naturalistic philosophers of the twentieth century, and also by most nonphilosophers when they think about death. On this view, as Schrag has put it, death is an "external and objective phenomenon,"[36] it is "simply a natural and empirical happening which comes to man at the completion of his life."[37] This "external" view is typically represented by the saying of Epicurus, "when I am, death is not and when death is, I am not." It is also implicit in the "common" notion of "death as that which results when one takes a dose of sulfuric acid, or drowns himself, or goes to sleep in an atmosphere of coal gas."[38] Such an "external" point of view of death is radically defective. "Classical paganism," Schrag tells us, "never arrives at a *genuine understanding* of the *existential reality* of death." Like "Hegel's objective idealism" it fails to achieve "subjective penetration" of death. The same is true of the everyday conception of death: "In our common, everyday, levelled understanding, what is existentially involved in dying fails to become transparent."[39] Viewing death as an "external fact" does not yield a "proper understanding."[40] The assumption that it is "simply a natural and empirical happening" is "*false.*"[41] William Barrett is in total agreement with this assessment of the "everyday understanding" of death. People "usually think of death as a fact in the world . . . it is something out there in the world as yet external to me."[42] This is a mistake: "Death is not a public fact out there in the world."[43] In opposition to this external view we are assured that Kierkegaard, Heidegger and other existentialists have achieved a proper understanding of death. They have done so by "interiorizing" death, to quote Schrag, by showing that death is an "interior possibility of the human self as concern or passion."[44] "Existentialist thinkers agree that death can be elucidated and described as a constitutive structure in man's situationality."[45] Heidegger in particular has developed an "ontology of death" in which "death is '*interiorized*' as a mode of existence itself."[46] Thanks to Heidegger, writes Father Demske, we realize that death is an "*internal* existential structure of the being of Dasein."[47] "Death," furthermore, "is not an event which puts an end to life . . . it does not lie in the future, but in the here and now, affecting every act in which existence is realized."[48] "Death as an existential is . . . a mode of being, a way to be, in fact *the* way in which Dasein exists."[49] "Death," according to Glenn Gray, "is a phenomenon within life" and he adds that "if it is taken into life in a personal way, it will effect a revolution in our behavior."[50] "Death," writes Father Boros, "is a *fundamental modality of living.*"[51] "The peculiar thing," Barrett remarks, is that "my death will never be a fact in the world for me." He goes on to observe that he will never read his own obituary and tells us that he regards this as a "very significant fact." Since death is not something "out there in the world," it is an "interior possibility,"[52] it is "something that happens *within* my own existence."[53]

How is the feat of "interiorizing" death accomplished? How is it shown that death is not external, but "internal," that it is "a mode of life?" This result, which on the face of it seems quite remarkable, is obtained by an analysis of what are claimed to be the different senses of the word "end" and the corresponding senses of "dying." It is "urgent," Heidegger tells us, to "ask *in what sense, if any, death must be conceived as the ending of Dasein*" (BT, p. 289, Heidegger's italics). To answer this question it is necessary to discuss the different senses of "ending." Schrag, who goes into somewhat more detail here than Heidegger, observes that "to come to an end commonly means to cease," adding however that " 'ceasing to be' has different modifications."[54] One such "modification" or sense is illustrated by Heidegger's own example—"the rain has stopped." Schrag gives the example of the end of the summer. Here we have "disappearance"—that which has ended, the rain or the summer is, in Heidegger's special terminology, "no longer present-at-hand" (BT, p. 289). In another sense, ending means completion. An artist has come to the end of his work when he has completed a painting "with the last stroke of the brush" (BT, p. 289). A further "modification" of ending is provided by cases where work will never be completed, in Schrag's words, "as when construction of a canal stops because the soil through which it must be cut proves too swampy."[55] A fourth modification is exemplified when something is used up, for example, a supply of gasoline or when we come to the end of a loaf of bread. Heidegger mentions another case which is significantly different from all those listed so far. If we come to the end of the road, this does not imply that the road has disappeared. Unlike the gasoline that has been used up, the bread that has been eaten or the rain that has stopped, the road continues to exist. "Such an ending," writes Heidegger, "does not make the road disappear, but . . . is determinative for the road as this one, which is present-at-hand" (BT, p. 289). There is some talk about "fulfillment" at this stage. It is not clear whether

Heidegger regards fulfillment as a "mode" of what he calls "fertigwerden" which M-R translate as "finishedness" and which in ordinary German simply means "completion." "Fulfilling," Heidegger writes, "is a mode of 'finishedness,' and is founded upon it." However, both he and Schrag insist—and rightly so—that ending in the sense of finishedness or completion does not necessarily involve fulfillment. "A project," to quote Schrag, "may end in the sense of being completed and yet be evaluated as either fulfilled or unfulfilled, as when we say that a performance ended well or ended poorly." [56]

In which of these senses does the death of Dasein constitute its end? In none of them. Many readers will be familiar with the basic distinction which Heidegger makes between Dasein on the one hand and entities that are ready-to-hand and present-at-hand on the other. This distinction is similar to the one between persons and things which is found in many nonexistentialists and it closely corresponds to Sartre's distinction between the *pour-soi* and the *en-soi*. Human beings have certain characteristics which are not possessed by inanimate objects or by plants and animals; and they are called Daseins to indicate their possession of these characteristics. Now, it is Heidegger's contention that the senses, modes or modifications of "ending" previously enumerated apply only to non-Daseins. Human beings are radically different from bread, paintings, roads, and the rain; and their end is radically different from the end of all these other entities:

> By none of these modes of ending can death be suitably characterized as the "end" of Dasein. If dying, as Being-at-an-end, were understood in the sense of an ending of the kind we have discussed, then Dasein would thereby be treated as something present-at-hand or ready-at-hand. In death, Dasein has not been fulfilled nor has it simply disappeared; it has not become finished nor is it wholly at one's disposal as something ready-to-hand. (p. 289, Heidegger's italics)

The "modifications of ending" so far discussed, in Schrag's words, "are not applicable to the unique Being of *Dasein* and hence cannot be used to characterize death as the end of his being-in-the world."

In what sense is death the end of Dasein? To answer this question we must briefly explain one of the key-notions of BT—"existentiality" or "running-ahead" ("vorlaufen"), what Schrag calls "protention." Human beings, according to Heidegger, are always "ahead" of themselves in the sense that they are and cannot help being concerned about their future. To explain the behavior or motion of inanimate objects and most, if not all, living things other than man, we need not take into account their concern for the future since they have no such concern. In the case of human beings, on the other hand, we cannot understand their *present* behavior or states without taking into account their concern for the future. Perhaps I should remark in passing that, although I object to various uses to which this notion is put by Heidegger, I do not at all dispute the fact that human beings are characterized by existentiality or "vorlaufen." If we keep in mind this universal characteristic of vorlaufen, Heidegger maintains, we shall discover the peculiar sense, radically different from all the other senses, in which death is the end of Dasein:

> The "ending" which we have in view when we speak of death, does not signify Dasein's Being-at-an-end but a *Being-towards-the end* of this entity." (p. 289, Heidegger's italics)

> *Death is*, as Dasein's end, *in* the Being of this entity *towards* its end. (p. 303, my italics of "in," otherwise Heidegger's italics)

It is in the "protentional character of Dasein" or its "running-ahead," Schrag tells us, "that the phenomenon of death is disclosed." This yields an "existential understanding" of death and "existentially understood, death does not signify a being-at-the-end." The "existentialist clarification of the meaning of the end" allows us to regard "death as being-unto-the-end."[57] "For the subjective thinker," death "is a present reality."[58] "Death is a mode of human concern . . . in which the transitoriness of existence is disclosed."[59]

Heidegger appears to believe that, in a quite literal sense, a human being *is* already its future, its "not-yet"; and thus he finds no difficulty in concluding that Dasein's end is already present while he is alive:

> Just as Dasein *is* already its "not-yet," and is its "not-yet" constantly as long as it is, it *is* already its end too. (p. 289, Heidegger's italics)

> Death "is not something to which Dasein ultimately comes only in its demise. In Dasein, as being towards its death, its own uttermost "not-yet" has already been included." (p. 303)

> Dasein, furthermore, "stretches *itself* along in such a way that its own Being is constituted in advance as a stretching along." (p. 426)

In this way, by means of running-ahead and "stretching" ("erstrecken"), Dasein can encompass its entire future. It can "take in advance" ("vorwegnehmen") the rest of its life and it can thus catch up with ("einholen") its own death:

> Since running-ahead to the possibility which is not to be outstripped discloses also all the possibilities which lie ahead of that possibility [meaning all future events that will happen before one's death], this running-ahead includes the possibility of taking *the whole* of Dasein in advance. (BT, p. 309, G 264, Heidegger's italics)

Needless to say, this "amalgamation" of present and future has the wholehearted endorsement of various of Heidegger's disciples. "The not-yet element of human existence," in the words of Gelven, "is something that is already there. Dasein is, in a very genuine sense, already its not-yet." "Dasein's 'not-yet death'," furthermore, "is already available for inquiry in a living and existing Dasein."[60] Similarly, Schrag assures us that "the existential future is *already* present . . . nor is the future a thing which will become real during the 'course of time' at a later date. The future is already real . . . ."[61] Again: "In existential anticipation (vorlaufen) the future is brought into the present."[62] "Dasein as ecstatic existence is stretched out into . . . a future in which he *already* is."[63] "The future," according to Glenn Gray,

> can be liberated if it is conceived as part of the present . . . the future will be seen to belong to the present in a fundamental way . . . the future must be regarded in a new way, as part of the existential moment . . . we understand the term "future" as a dimension of the present.[64]

Heidegger repeatedly remarks that *all* human beings are dying *all the time*. "Factically," he writes, "one's own Dasein is always dying" (p. 292). "Factically, Dasein is dying as long as it exists" (p. 295). And most fully: "Dasein is dying factically and indeed constantly, as long as it has not yet come to its demise" (p. 303). Clearly, these statements are another way of expressing the doctrine that human life is being-towards-death. When Heidegger asserts that all human beings are dying all the time he is not referring to the fact that cells are constantly dying in human bodies. Heidegger is not concerned with such biological details. That the life of human beings is being-towards-death is something that could have been known (and I suppose Heidegger would say was in fact known, though not in the explicit way in which BT codifies this knowledge) long before biologists knew that cells are constantly dying and even long before the existence of cells had been discovered. Biological facts Heidegger would classify as "ontic." That human life is being-towards-death is something "ontological." Although the meaning of "ontological" is never clearly explained, it is apparent that Heidegger would not regard a characteristic of human beings as "ontological" if it were not somehow necessarily connected with or part of the constitution of their humanity; and being-towards-death is essentially connected with their humanity while any detailed facts discovered by biologists are not.

The remarks of the preceding paragraph tell us what "dying" in the existential or ontological sense does not mean. They do not tell us what it does mean; and I do not think that any of the passages I quoted from Heidegger or Schrag or Demske spell out very clearly the content of "being-towards-death." To discover this we have to determine the necessary and sufficient conditions which an entity must satisfy in order for its life to be characterized as being-towards-death. Clearly one condition is that an entity should die in the biological sense. As I understand Heidegger, the life of human beings would definitely not be being-towards-death if they lived forever in the biological sense. However, this condition is clearly not enough. For Heidegger and his followers are emphatic that the life of plants and animals is not being-towards-death although they also die in the biological sense.[65]

What is true of human beings and not true of plants and animals in virtue of which we attribute being-towards-death to the former and not to the latter? Some of Heidegger's remarks in this connection are enigmatic, but various of his followers have been more explicit and it is I think fairly easy to see the kind of thing he has in mind. "Non-human organisms," in the words of Father Demske, "actually come to an end, but assume no attitude or relation to their cessation and thus have no 'being-unto-the-end.' "[66] Similarly, in a passage previously quoted, Schrag speaks of being-towards-death as a mode of "concern." Human beings, to begin with, know that they are going to die in a sense in which animals and plants do not know this. It is often said that animals have an instinctive fear of death, but even if this is so it is not the same thing as explicit awareness of death; and it is certainly not the same thing as, what Heidegger is specially concerned with when he talks about anxiety as contrasted with fear, namely the realization that death means total extinction or "utter nullity." The knowledge human beings have of their mortality has or may have all kinds of significant effects on their behavior and on their emotions. In short, unlike animals and plants, they think about their death, they are concerned about their death, and, sometimes at least, they act in ways in which they would not have acted if they had not known their own mortality. It should be emphasized that, according to Heidegger, being-towards-death is not something we can help. It is not in any sense within our volitional control. What is within our volitional control is whether our being-towards-death is to be "authentic" or "inauthentic." "Dasein has always *decided* itself in one way or another" (p. 303, my italics). Most commonly, Dasein's comportment towards death is of the inauthentic kind. "Proximally and for the most part Dasein covers up its ownmost Being-towards-death, fleeing *in the face of it*" (p. 295, Heidegger's italics). This "everyday falling evasion *in the face of* death is an *inauthentic* Being-towards-death" (p. 303, Heidegger's italics). Such evasive comportment, however, is no less a form of Being-towards-death than the authentic variety:

> In thus falling and fleeing *in the face of* death, Dasein's everydayness attests that the very "they" itself already has the definite character of *Being-towards-death*, even when it is not explicitly engaged in "thinking about death." (pp. 298–99, Heidegger's italics)

Death is "constantly an issue for Dasein" even in "average everydayness" (p. 299). "Everyday Dasein," no less than authentic Dasein, "*is towards its end*—that is to say, is constantly coming to grips with its death, though in a 'fugitive' manner" (p. 303, Heidegger's italics). Being-towards-death is not something which Dasein "procures for itself . . . occasionally in the course of its Being" (p. 295). It characterizes Dasein right from the start. "It belongs essentially to Dasein's thrownness, which reveals itself in a state-of-mind in one way or another" (*ibid.*).

The above account makes it clear that all that is meant by the Heideggerian statement that human life is being-towards-death is, first, that human beings die, and, second, that unlike plants and animals they know and are, fugitively or nonfugitively, concerned about their death. The objection to this statement is not that it is false, but that it is a platitude. Heidegger and his disciples announce this doctrine with the kind of fanfare that is usually reserved for a major contribution to human knowledge. The impression is given that it constitutes a great discovery or an important insight; and we are given to understand that Heidegger has refuted or at least corrected the view of the pagan thinkers of antiquity, of naturalistic philosophers and of ordinary people, that death is an "external" fact. It is easy to show that Heidegger's doctrine is not a discovery of anything, that it embodies no significant insight, and that it does not in any way refute or correct the view that death is an "external" fact. It states what are for the most part exceedingly familiar facts which are not disputed by pagans, naturalists or ordinary people, but it states them in pretentious and fantastically misleading language. We are offered a platitude, accompanied by a slurring of certain elementary distinctions and a set of perverse redefinitions.

To show the emptiness of the Heideggerian doctrine and the perverse character of Heidegger's verbal games it will be helpful to insist on a simple distinction which no sane person disputes. This is the distinction between death (in the ordinary sense) and knowledge of and concern about death. Death in the ordinary sense is *not* a "way to be, " a "mode of human concern" or a "mode of life." It is the absence of life. *Knowledge and concern* about death may be a mode of life or aspects or constituents of a mode of life. While writing these words I am alive. My death is something which has not yet taken place. My concern about my death occurs while I am alive and it precedes my death. It will be convenient to use the symbol "d_o" to refer to death in the ordinary sense and to use "c_d" to refer to knowledge and concern about one's death. We are told by Heidegger and his followers that "existentially" and "properly" understood, death is being-toward-death. This "existential" and "proper" understanding of death is supposed to "interiorize" death and make it into a "present" fact. It allegedly shows the falseness or inadequacy of the naturalist view. In effect Heidegger and his followers propose to use the word "death" in a drastically new sense to mean c_d and not d_o. If anybody wishes to talk in this way, there is no law to stop him, but one can point out that it accomplishes nothing, or nothing of any value. Referring to c_d by the word "death" does not amount to a discovery of anything. Nor does it refute or correct the Epicurean viewpoint. In declaring "when death is, I am not," Epicurus spoke about d_o and not about c_d. To refute Epicurus d_o and not c_d would have to be shown to be an "interior" and "present" reality; and this has not been done. Epicurus did indeed advocate an attitude towards death that is very different from the one that appears to be endorsed by Heideggerians. However, it is safe to assume that he was neither ignorant nor oblivious of the fact that, unlike plants and animals, human beings know and are concerned about their death.

Contrary to Schrag's claim, Heidegger's redefinition is not "the elucidation" or "clarification" of anything whatever. On the contrary,.the undeniable difference between d_o and c_d has been slurred over and obscured. Heidegger himself cannot, of course, do without this distinction. Thus he speaks of Dasein's "uttermost and unoutstrippable possibility" and he says a great deal about the "anxiety" that is involved in an "authentic" approach to this uttermost and unoutstrippable possibility. The uttermost and unoutstrippable possibility is *death* and not *being-towards*-death; and if death were not distinguished from being-towards-death there would not be anything for the authentic approach to be an approach to. Being-towards-death is being towards *death in the ordinary sense*, i.e., towards d_o. It is *not* being towards c_d, towards death in the new redefined or existential sense; it is being-towards-*death* and not being-towards-*being-towards*-death.

Similar comments apply to the contention of Schrag, Barrett, Gray and other Heideggerians that death is not a public fact, but something that happens "within" a person's existence. Barrett observes that his death will not be a fact in the world *for him* and he regards it as highly significant that he will not be around to read his obituary. All this is totally irrelevant to the point at issue between Heideggerians and Epicurus. That Barrett will not be able to witness his death or that he will not read his obituary does not have the slightest tendency to show that his death will not be a public fact. Barrett's death, when it occurs, *will* be a public fact—it will be observed or at any rate it could in principle become the object of the observation of people who will be alive at the time. Let us divide the history of the world into three phases—the phase coinciding with Barrett's life, the pre-Barrett phase and the post-Barrett phase. During the pre-Barrett phase a multitude of public facts existed although Barrett was unable to observe them. Similarly, in the post-Barrett phase there will be vast number of facts (other than his own death) whose public character will not in any way be undone by Barrett's inability to perceive them. The same is obviously true of Barrett's death. What is or may be a "private" fact, what happens "within" a person's existence while he is alive is not death, but thoughts and concern about death.[67]

The emptiness of the Heideggerian doctrine can be seen very clearly when we take a closer look at Heidegger's assertion that all human beings, including young people who are in the best of health and leading the safest possible life, are always dying. This certainly sounds like a discovery. It *appears* to conflict with commonly accepted beliefs, but this appearance is deceptive. Let us assume that Samuel Blau is a man of fifty-five who is dying (in the ordinary sense) of some dreadful disease like stomach cancer. Let us suppose that he has a son, Bobby, aged twenty, who appears to be in the best of health. The family physician, Dr. Adelman, is a convert to Heidegger's philosophy. Bobby has a regular check-up and Dr. Adelman finds nothing wrong with his health. Nevertheless, Dr. Adelman tells the mother, "I am sorry to inform you that not only your husband, but your son Bobby too is dying." The poor startled woman calls out in dismay "but he looks so well and he is so young—don't tell me he too has cancer." To this Dr. Adelman replies: "No, no—he does not have cancer, he is in the best of health, but you must realize that he is going to die eventually, that he knows he is going to die and that he has some attitude, authentic or inauthentic—I am not sure which—to his death." Bobby's mother, if she kept her composure, could appropriately reply, "It is a relief to hear that Bobby is dying only in this special sense of yours. I just wish my husband too were dying only in this sense." Dr. Adelman's statement that Bobby too is dying is a platitude whose platitudinous nature is not at once apparent because is is using a familiar word in an unfamiliar sense. Heidegger *seems* to be saying that everybody at all times is mortally ill like Samuel Blau. This indeed would be a tremendous and a shattering discovery, but it is false; and it is *not* what Heidegger really asserts. The Heideggerian physician seems to but has not in fact made a surprising discovery about Bobby; and Heidegger seems to, but has not added to our knowledge or understanding of anything when he announces that everybody is always dying.

Heidegger's argument that we do not mean the same by "end" when we speak of the end of a human life, as we do when we speak of the end of the life of a plant or an animal or the end of an inanimate object, is totally fallacious. When we speak of the end of the latter kind of entity we mean that it ceases or has ceased to exist. We allegedly do not mean this when we speak of the end of a human life. The argument to support this conclusion rests on the contention that, unlike the other entities, human beings are Daseins—they are characterized by such features or capacities as running-ahead or existentiality. This is true, but it does not prove Heidegger's point. From the fact that human beings are Daseins it does not at once follow that a category applicable to non-Daseins is not also applicable to them; and it also does not follow that when the same word is predicated of both, it does not mean the same thing in both cases. The category of causation clearly applies to non-Daseins. It *may* be true, but it certainly does not automatically follow that, because human beings are Daseins, their actions are not caused in the same sense in which we speak of the causation of physical events and purely biological phenomena. In fact, Heidegger and Schrag notwithstanding, it is perfectly clear that when we speak of the end of a human life we use the word "end" in exactly the same sense in which we use it when we speak of the end of non-Daseins. When a house has been wrecked or burned down its existence has come to an end. It has ceased to exist and, barring survival after death which is not what Heidegger and Schrag are concerned with, exactly the same is true when a human being has died. The fact that the subjects of these statements are different from one another in all kinds of ways does not mean that the word "end" is predicated of them in different senses. Of course, if one *re*defines "end" to mean knowledge and concern about the end, i.e., "being-towards-the-end," as Heidegger eventually does, then Dasein does end in a sense in which non-Daseins do not end. But this is not an elucidation of anything. It is just the same verbal trick which we already exposed in the case of the word "death."

Some Heideggerians seem uneasily aware of the emptiness of the doctrine under discussion and they try to shore it up by alluding to certain additional empirical facts. Thus Father Demske quotes a passage from Karl Rahner in which the latter observes that throughout life we are "continually disappointed, ceaselessly piercing through realities into their nothingness, continually narrowing the possibilities of free life through our actual decisions and actual life . . . we die throughout life and what we call death is really the end of death, the death of death."[68] Demske also quotes certain statements made by Tanabe, the Japanese Heideggerian to whom I referred at the beginning of this article. Tanabe repeatedly remarks that man "lives dying" and also "dies living," which Demske interprets to mean that "during the whole of life man is constantly forced to give things up, to deny himself, do without things, offer himself."[69] To this it must be replied that, in declaring human life to be being-towards-death, Heidegger is *not* asserting any of the facts mentioned by Rahner and Tanabe. Presumably Heidegger would not deny that all or almost all human beings are occasionally disappointed, that they have to make sacrifices and deny themselves various satisfactions, but this is a purely contingent matter and would be classified by Heidegger as something "ontic." It is *at least* logically conceivable that a human being might go through life without once being disappointed and without having to deny himself anything. Such a person's life, as Heidegger uses the expression, would nevertheless be an instance of being-towards-death. It would be so because, in spite of his freedom from disappointments and the absence of sacrifices, he too would die and he too would know that he was going to die and adopt some kind of attitude towards his death.

A final word about the Heideggerian notion that the future *is* in the present, that I am "already" all my not-yets including my death. Heidegger is evidently under the spell of certain pictures—pictures associated with the words "vorlaufen," "erstrecken," "einholen" and "vorwegnehmen." I can stretch out and reach the salt shaker while I remain sitting on my chair. If I am in the front-row of a procession I can run ahead and thus be in advance of the position I would be occupying if I had stayed in line. Heidegger believes that in the same way I can stretch or run into the future while I am still in the present. If this were possible then I *could* now be my not-yet and I could also get my death into the present. But it is not possible. Heideggerians can take this sort of talk seriously only as long as it is conducted on a totally abstract level, unrelieved by a single concrete illustration. I can now, in 1979, think about 1980 and other future years, but I cannot literally live in them. I can *metaphorically* "run ahead" and "stretch into" 1980, but all this means is that I can think about, prepare for, be hopeful or afraid of 1980. I cannot literally run ahead or stretch into 1980; and as we saw, it is a literal running ahead that is needed for Heidegger's purpose of "interiorizing" death.[70] If I will in fact die ten years after these words are written, I *cannot* literally run ahead, stretch out and catch up with my death. In any nonperverse sense it is *not* true that I am my end while I am alive; and more generally it is not true that I am already all my not-yets. No amount of verbal juggling will make it otherwise.

4. Death as our "Capital Possibility"

Ferrater Mora, a Spanish admirer of Heidegger, has referred to Heidegger's view that "the being of Dasein is a being unto death" as a "famous contention."[71] In the light of our remarks in the preceding section it may be questioned whether the statements Heidegger makes in this connection qualify as a "contention," but it is probably true that, of all the many phrases he has coined, none has been picked up by more people than "Sein zum Tode." However, both he and several of his disciples regard another of his "contentions" as the real climax of his investigation into the nature of death. This is his repeated assertion that death is a "possibility"—possibility as opposed to actuality. Most people, we are given to understand, have an incorrect attitude toward death.because they regard it as an actuality, because in various ways they try to "weaken" its possibility. Heidegger, on the other hand, as a result of his great insight that death is a possibility and not an actuality, has shown "the correct attitude of man toward death." These are the words of William A. Luijpen a Dutch enthusiast, who proceeds to claim—something Heidegger himself also asserts—that in characterizing death as possibility, Heidegger has "unveiled" the "true meaning of death."[72] In this and the next section I will try to explain and evaluate these claims as well as some of the related pronouncements of certain of Heidegger's followers.

Throughout *Being and Time* Heidegger speaks of death as a possibility. It is our uttermost, our unoutstrippable or unsurpassable, our ownmost and our non-relational possibility. It would be unfair to say that Heidegger never explains what he means when he describes death as a "possibility." After speaking in this way for some twenty-five pages, close to the end of the chapter on death, he finally explains what he means; and it turns out that he means neither what the word means in any of its ordinary senses *nor* what he himself had meant by it throughout BT. The new use, it turns out, is *utterly and totally* different from all these other uses.

Something must be said at this stage about the special sense of "possibility" Heidegger had introduced earlier in BT in which he uses the word throughout the book *except* when talking about death. Dasein,

Heidegger writes, "determines its own character as the kind of entity it is, and it does so in every case in terms of a possibility which it itself *is* and which it understands" (pp. 303–304, Heidegger's italics). "Possibility" in this sense is to be "sharply distinguished both from empty logical possibility and from the contingency of something present-at-hand" (p. 183). Evidently Heidegger uses "possibility" to refer to the alternatives which we can choose or, more precisely, which we *know* ourselves to be capable of choosing. "Dasein is such that in every case it has understood . . . that it is to be thus or thus. As such understanding it 'knows' *what* it is capable of" (p. 184, Heidegger's italics), where the "knowing" is of a non-theoretical kind. None of this is terribly clear and, as usual, not a single illustration is provided. However, one can in a general way see what Heidegger has in mind. Macquarrie has in several places explained what this sense of "possibility" comes to. Thus, in a glossary, appended to his book, *Martin Heidegger*, he writes: "Possibility, in Heidegger's thought, does not mean just any contingency that may happen, but refers to the open future for which the Dasein can decide."[73] In another book, also largely devoted to Heidegger, he emphasizes that "by possibility Heidegger does not mean simply a contingency that might happen to me, but a genuine possibility of existence which man may in a certain way choose for himself."[74] Similarly, Demske explains that "in Heidegger's existential phenomenology possibility indicates what Dasein can be, do or become."[75] "Possibility" here clearly refers to an action or a strategy or a mode of life (something like Sartre's "fundamental project") which a human being may adopt or choose. Heroism or cowardice, I believe, would be examples of a person's or at least of some people's possibilities in this sense. I add the qualification "some people's" because Heidegger is very emphatic that the freedom of choice he favours is not to be confused with "a free-floating potentiality-for-Being in the sense of 'liberty of indifference'." (p. 183) Human beings know themselves to be able to choose between *certain* alternatives, but "thrownness" restricts the range of what in a given situation is possible.

Now, when Heidegger maintains that death is a person's possibility, he is *not* using "possibility" in the sense just explained. It appears that Heidegger has been misunderstood in this connection not only by Sartre, who is here writing in opposition to Heidegger, but also by his devoted followers. Not noticing Heidegger's shift from the sense of "possibility" explained in the preceding paragraph to the totally different sense I have yet to explain, they have delivered some altogether startling pronouncements, which, as it ultimately turns out, are not at all implied in Heidegger's doctrine that death is a possibility. I have in mind here what may be called the "golden opportunity" view of death and the even more amazing notion that death is the "crown" of our lives. Heidegger repeatedly refers to death as our "ausgezeichnete Möglichkeit" which M-R translate, weakly and inaccurate-

ly, as "our distinctive possibility" and for which a more accurate translation
would be "splendid" or "distinguished possibility."[76] This and similar
statements have apparently been taken to mean that death is something like
our golden opportunity. Glenn Gray speaks of death as "life's greatest
possibility" as well as our "great privilege and challenge" which is something
to be "welcomed."[77] Luijpen, after remarking correctly, though not very
originally, that human life would not be "what it is without death," proceeds
to affirm that "death is the mode of potential being which is most proper to
man," it is nothing less, in fact, than "the most proper possibility of his
existence."[78] Not to be outdone, Macquarrie calls it our "capital
possibility."[79] These expressions suggest that death is like the opportunity
that comes to an understudy for a great singer when the latter is suddenly
taken ill. Lotte Lehmann had her great opportunity, her "capital possibility,"
when the renowned Marie Gutheil-Schoder could not sing the role of the
Composer in the Vienna premiere of *Ariadne auf Naxos*. Father Demske,
after telling us that death is "the possibility of all possibilities," finally
reaches the remarkable conclusion that it is the "crown and culmination of
human life."[80] Using almost the same language, the German writer Paul
Hühnerfeld, concludes that "death becomes the crowning ("die Krönung") of
. . . life."[81] I do not think I overstated the case when I referred to such
pronouncements as startling. Except when bent on suicide or in the midst of
terrible suffering, we do *not* normally regard death as something wonderful
that is to be welcomed, but on the contrary as something to be avoided and
put off as long as possible. I believe that the conductor of the Vienna
premiere of *Ariadne auf Naxos* was Franz Schalk, a sane and kindly man,
who took a fatherly interest in Lotte Lehmann. I cannot imagine him saying
to her, even in jest, "Lottchen—your greatest opportunity has come. If you
were still alive tomorrow, you could sing the Composer in place of Gutheil-
Schoder. However, you will be dead before the day is up—this is your capital
possibility." Wild and Schrag do not speak of death as "the crown and
culmination of our lives," but it appears that they too are guided by Heidegger's initial use of "possibility" when they declare that death is a "task" or an
"act." Death, writes Schrag, is "not simply a contingent happening," it is "a
task or an existential project."[82] Rightly conceived, "death becomes a task or
a responsibility which Dasein must assume."[83] In a similar vein Wild declares
that death "is an *actual act* to be lived through by an individual alone."[84]

It will be of some interest to evaluate these "opportunity," "crown" and
"task" notions of death before we follow Heidegger into his explanation of
what he does mean by speaking of death as a possibility. To this end it will be
helpful to distinguish between what I will call (a) deadness, (b) the death-
moment, (c) death-producing events, and (d) dying. First of all, a few words
about the distinction between (a) and (b). By "death-moment" I shall mean
the first moment following the conclusion of a person's life. A doctor may
report that his patient, Samuel Blau, died at 5:04 on Monday, January 11,

1979. This would be Samuel Blau's death-moment. From then on, for all eternity, he will be dead. This fact which can be truly asserted of Samuel Blau is what I will mean by his "deadness." It is tempting, but also very misleading, to speak of Samuel Blau's "state" of deadness and I am deliberately avoiding such language (I will return to this point in the next section). By "death-producing event" I shall mean the kind of thing that would be mentioned as the cause of death in a newspaper obituary or in a biography—e.g., cancer, a heart attack, suicide, a plane crash, being run over by a car, etc. Such an account frequently differs from a detailed medical report which would list the *immediate* physiological antecedents as cause of death. I am using the word "event" in a very broad sense here so that it would include both actions and conditions which are not normally described as actions. Suicide would be an example of an action which is a death-producing event and so would a dangerous attempt to rescue somebody from a fire. Cancer, heart attacks or being assassinated are death-producing events which we do not normally regard as actions. My use of "death-producing event" is not at all precise, but for our limited purpose no further explanation is necessary. Finally, by "dying" I will mean the phase in the life of an individual between the beginning of the death-producing event and his death-moment. In the case of a person who is killed in a plane crash this would be a very short period. In the case of somebody dying of a disease like cancer it could be an extended period. I believe that this roughly coincides with the everyday use of the word. Like the latter, it is far from precise, but again this will not affect any of the issues in our subsequent discussion.

Let us now return to what I called the golden opportunity- and the crown- notions of death and let us concentrate on Demske's statement that death is the "crown and culmination" of human life. It should be noted that Demske is asserting this of *every* human life. It should also be remembered that, although he is a believer in immortality, Father Demske is not in this context referring to survival of any kind. He is expounding and defending the views of Heidegger. Now, it is not false but *meaningless* to speak either of deadness or the death-moment as the "crown and culmination" of a human life. In any intelligible sense, the culmination of a person's life must be an event or a sequence of events *in* his life. It must be something occurring while he is alive. It makes sense and it is probably true that the crown and culmination of Winston Churchill's life was his leadership of Great Britain during the war against Hitler, but it makes no sense to say that the crown and culmination of his life was his death-moment on a certain day in January, 1965, or his deadness since that time. It is not meaningless to speak of the death-producing event in a person's life or of his dying as crown and culmination. Such a statement is not meaningless, but, asserted as a universal proposition, it is quite certainly false. In Rossellini's *Il Generale Della Rovere*, the main character, Bardone, is a small-time crook in an Italian town who is mistaken for the leader of the Resistance against the Fascists. He courageously goes to his death, when he could have escaped such a fate by revealing his true identity. It may well be true that his refusal to save himself *was* the crown of his life. Again, some people whose lives were undistinguished by any high-minded deeds, showed remarkable courage and equanimity during their terminal illness. There is a moving illustration of this in *Der Tod des Kleinbürgers* by the great Austrian poet and novelist, Franz Werfel. The story is about the last days of Karl Fiala, a retired janitor, who lost his modest savings in the inflation that followed the first World War. Fiala has an epileptic son who is unable to hold a job. His one desire is to make sure that after his death the son should not be committed to a mental institution. He has taken out life insurance which would adequately provide for his widow and son, but the premiums are conditional on Fiala's not dying until he reaches the age of sixty-five. Two months before his sixty-fifth birthday he becomes mortally ill and is moved to a hospital room reserved for patients who are expected to die within a matter of hours. Against all predictions and to the annoyance of the doctors and nurses he refuses to die and exceeds his goal by two days. Throughout the last two days he was heard to mumble "es ist vollbracht." Fiala had been a meek and humble man, completely dominated by his wife and her sister. His final struggle was the only heroic episode in his life. It is arguable that in such a case the individual's dying is indeed the crown of his life. However, as a universal proposition, Demske's statement is surely untenable. Clarence Darrow's life had many highlights, but there was nothing at all interesting about his life during his final illness. Similarly, Winston Churchill died of complications from a fall, after several years of physical and mental decline. When Father Demske claims that death is the crown and culmination of human life, he is not, it seems clear, intending to assert the false but intelligible proposition that either the death-producing event or the person's dying is the climax of every human life. He is speaking of deadness just, as we shall see, Heidegger is speaking of deadness when he declares death to be a possibility. Father Demske is speaking of deadness; and hence his pronouncement is not intelligible and false, but nonsense. Similar remarks apply to the golden-opportunity statements and the statements that death is a task or an act. It is nonsense to speak of deadness or death-moments as acts or tasks; and it will also in most contexts be absurd to speak of them as "capital possibilities." It is not necessarily nonsense and it may in certain cases be true that a death-producing event is a task and a capital possibility; and the same holds for "dying." As universal propositions, however, these statements are quite certainly false.

5. The "Possibility of the Impossibility of Existing"

Let us now return to Heidegger himself. The chapter on death in BT consists of eight sections. After having told us throughout the preceding sections

that death is a "possibility," Heidegger finally realizes in the last section that
his use of the word in this context may be easily misunderstood. Before telling
us what he does mean he discusses in some detail three possible misunderstandings. First Heidegger notes that his statement that "Being-
towards-death is Being-towards-a-possibility" may suggest that he is thinking
of death as a possibility which can and perhaps should be "actualized" the
way in which we might actualize a possible visit to the opera or a possible trip
to Paris. Heidegger is emphatic that in calling death Dasein's "possibility" he
does not use the word in this way and, furthermore, that the attitude he
recommends towards death is in no way like our attitude towards a possibility
which we are trying to actualize. The latter attitude which he calls "concern-
fully Being out for something possible" has "a tendency to *annihilate the
possibility* of the possible by making it available to us." (p. 305, Heidegger's
italics). Such an attitude "weakens" the possibility of death and Heidegger is
concerned to do the opposite. In any event, if he meant by "possibility"
something that we can actualize he would in effect be recommending suicide;
and this is not what he is doing:

> To concern oneself with actualizing what is thus possible would have to signify,
> "bringing about one's demise." But if this were done, Dasein would deprive itself
> of the very ground for an existing Being-towards-death.[85]

In his discussion of the two other misunderstandings, Heidegger does not
mention any further senses of "possibility" but instead he mentions two attitudes towards death which he may be taken to recommend and which he is
in fact eager to disavow. The first of these is "brooding" ("grübeln"). In
brooding "one 'thinks about death,' pondering over when and how this
possibility may perhaps be actualized" (p. 305). It is true that brooding does
not "fully take away" from death "its character as a possibility." However,
just as we weaken the possibility of the possible when we are trying to actualize it, so brooding, too, "weakens" the possibility of death by
"calculating how we are to have it at our disposal" (pp. 305–06). In this way
death "is to show as little as possible of its possibility" (p. 306). To achieve an
authentic being-towards-death we must do the exact opposite:

> Death must be understood *as a possibility*, it must be cultivated as a possibility,
> and we must *endure it as a possibility* in the way we comport ourselves toward it.
> (*Ibid.*, G, 261, Heidegger's italics)

Nor is "erwarten" (what M-R translate as "expecting") the right attitude;
and again for the same reason:

> To expect something possible is always to understand it and to "have" it with
> regard to whether and when and how it will be actually present-at-hand. (*Ibid.*)

If anything, it seems, expecting is worse than brooding as far as weakening or
falsifying the possibility of death is concerned. Expecting, Heidegger tells us

quite plausibly, "is essentially a *waiting for . . . actualization*" (*Ibid.*, Heidegger's italics). In expecting, he adds, "one leaps away from the possible and gets a foothold on the actual . . . by the very nature of expecting, the possible is drawn into the actual, arising out of the actual and returning to it" (*Ibid.*).

At this stage the reader may despair of ever discovering what Heidegger means when he speaks of death as "possibility" and what attitude, different from trying to bring about death, brooding over death, or expecting death, he champions. All possibilities, if I may revert to one of the ordinary senses of the word, seem to have been exhausted.[86] Not so. The right attitude and the clue to the "true nature" of the possibility of death is "vorlaufen in die Möglichkeit" which M-R misleadingly translate as "anticipation of the possibility" and which I shall translate very literally as "running ahead into the possibility." We already met "vorlaufen" or "running ahead" in Section 3 in connection with Heidegger's view that the future can be transported into the present. At first sight "running ahead" may not seem significantly different from "expecting," but Heidegger tells us that it involves an "understanding" which is absent in expecting. In the kind of "coming close" which is represented by "running ahead," one comes closer to death "understandingly." This does *not* "tend towards making available something actual" (p. 306). On the contrary,

> as one comes closer understandingly, the possibility of the possible just becomes "greater." *The closest closeness which one may have in Being towards death as a possibility, is as far as possible from anything actual.* (pp. 306–07, Heidegger's italics)

We have now arrived at the answer to the riddle. In this "closest closeness" the nature of the possibility becomes "unveiled." The "understanding penetrates into it" and reveals it "*as the possibility of the impossibility of any existence at all*" (p. 307, Heidegger's italics). In a later chapter this "possibility of the impossibility of existence" is identified with the "schlechthinnige Nichtigkeit" of Dasein which M-R translate as its "utter nullity" and which might perhaps be more idiomatically rendered as "total nothingness" (p. 354, G. 306). The unveiling reveals death as "the possibility of the impossibility of *every* way of comporting oneself towards anything, of *every* way of existing" (p. 307, my italics).

> As we "run ahead into the possibility," it "becomes 'ever greater,' that is to say, the possibility reveals itself to be 'such that it knows no measure at all, no more or less, but signifies the possibility of the measureless impossibility of existence'." (p. 307, G. 262).

It now becomes clear why Heidegger is so intent on using the word "possibility." Death is not an "actuality," not a state, but the absence of all states. Death is a possibility because it "gives Dasein nothing to be 'actualized,' nothing which Dasein, as actual, could itself *be*" (*Ibid.*, Heidegger's italics). If we regard death as a possibility we will not make the mistake of "picturing" (the word Heidegger uses is "ausmalen" which literally means "paint a content") it as an actuality.

What are we to say of this conclusion and the way in which Heidegger arrived at it? Primarily two things—first, if one agrees, as I do, that there is no survival, Heidegger is quite right in describing death as a *total* absence, and, second, that his use of the word "possibility" is fantastically misleading. Surely speaking of death as "possibility" when what and *all* that is meant is that death is the total *absence* of experiences and behavior, the annihilation of all consciousness, the impossibility of every way of comporting oneself, is carrying the misuse of language to the ultimate degree. The total absence of experiences and behavior is most emphatically *not* what we mean by "possibility" in any of its ordinary senses and it is *equally* not what Heidegger himself meant when he introduced the word "possibility" in his special sense to mean the actions or conduct or mode of life which a person may choose. No wonder that he has been misunderstood by his own followers and no wonder that his pronouncement sounds strange and is regarded by his uncritical worshippers, not simply as a statement of the unbeliever's view on the subject of survival, but as a remarkable and profound insight. If Heidegger had, from the start, used the proper language and simply spoken of death as total annihilation, there would have been no occasion for all the hocus pocus about the "closest closeness" to the "possibility of the possible" which becomes "ever greater." Equally, there would have been no occasion for posturing as a great discoverer who "unveils" and "understandingly penetrates" the nature of death. Instead, Heidegger might have given us the reasons—and there are very good ones—for supposing that death is really the end and that belief in survival is an illusion. Bertrand Russell reached the same result with less effort and without fear of being misunderstood in his essay, "What I Believe" in which he wrote, quite simply, "I believe that when I die I shall rot, and nothing of my ego will survive."[87]

When Heidegger talks about the "possibility of the impossibility of every way of existing," the word "possibility" is altogether superfluous. What makes death a "non-actuality" and thus a "possibility" in his strange special sense *is* the impossibility of every way of existing. This is what the possibility in the new sense *consists in*. The redundancy of "possibility" in the phrase "possibility of the impossibility of existing" is not at once apparent because the reader is apt to revert to the familiar sense in which "possibility" is contrasted with probability or certainty. It is "possible" but not certain that I will die five years from now. Heidegger is very definitely not using "possible" in *this* sense when characterizing death as a possibility. For Heidegger repeatedly insists—quite rightly, though not very originally—that death is a *certainty* and not just a possibility in *this* sense. However, the existence and familiarity of this ordinary sense tends to hide the redundancy of "possibility" in Heidegger's phrase "possibility of the impossibility of every way of existing." "Possibility" adds nothing here, or, rather, nothing but confusion.

If we ignore his continued employment of the word "possibility" even after it has become clear that he means nothing of the kind, Heidegger's final formulation is not without merit. If one grants that there is no survival then it is well to emphasize that death is an *utter* or *total* or *radical* absence. Our everyday language and the writings of poets are studded with images that make us, even those who are unbelievers, on occasions think of death as a form of rest or sleep or peace—a shadowy, low-grade form of consciousness. We, or some of us, have a tendency, as Heidegger puts it, to "paint a content" into our notion of death. In opposition to this tendency, it is well to emphasize that, if survival is a myth, death is not a form of rest or sleep, that it is not a low-grade form of consciousness, but the absence of all consciousness. Heidegger is right to speak of death as *"measureless* impossibility of existence." It is not just a partial absence like blindness or deafness or the loss of one's singing voice or paralysis in one part of one's body. It is the total absence of capacities and experiences. It is, as Heidegger puts it, the "impossibility of *every* way of comporting oneself towards anything, of *every* way of existing." There are grounds for saying that, at least for most people, blindness would be worse than deafness, that losing one's capacity to sing is not as terrible as becoming paralysed from the neck down. These losses are not "measureless," they are losses experienced by living individuals and involve states which can be compared. We cannot in the same way compare the absence of all states with any given state. In this sense we may agree that death is "measureless."

It will be helpful in some of our later discussions if I offer a slightly different formulation of what is sound in Heidegger's conclusion that death is "the possibility of the impossibility of every way of existing." Following Aristotle, several recent writers have distinguished between "actions" and "passions." An "action" in this sense is anything a person does, e.g., delivering a speech, playing a game of tennis, singing a song, calling an ambulance. A "passion" is anything which happens to a human being—the joy he feels when listening to beautiful music, the boredom he experiences when listening to a tedious lecture, or the pain he endures after suffering an accident. This distinction is not of course very precise, but it is one which all of us make in certain situations. Now, when people describe death as rest or sleep or peace, they have realized that death is not an "action," but, to the extent to which they are serious, they mistakenly regard it as a "passion"—presumably the most passive of all passions. However, if it is granted that there is no afterlife then, death, just like non-existence before birth, is neither an action nor a passion. If we introduce the word "state" to mean any action or passion, we can express our (and Heidegger's) point by saying that, unlike rest, sleep and peace, death is not a state.[88]

Readers of BT will be familiar with the fact that Heidegger never says anything simply and clearly if he can say it oddly, obscurely and ponderously; and I have no doubt that the desire to sound esoteric and original is part of the reason for his fantastic misuse of the word "possibility." There is also, however, a logical fallacy behind it. Heidegger evidently believes that if something that can be meaningfully talked about is not an "actuality" in the sense in which he is here using the word, then it must be a possibility. Death is not an actuality; hence it is a "possibility." This argument, which hovers in the background of Heidegger's discussion, calls for two comments. In the first place, the word "actuality" is ambiguous. There is a sense in which Heidegger is right to deny that death is something actual, but there is another and perfectly natural sense in which it is (or becomes) an actuality. Jefferson and President Kennedy, to take two familiar cases, are actually dead. It is *a fact* that they are dead. Their death has *actually* occurred. My own death has not yet occurred but at some time in the future it will occur, and when it occurs it will be an actuality. Let us call this the "occurrence" sense of "actuality" or "actuality$_o$." I already explained what Heidegger means when he says that death is not an actuality. He does not deny that it actually occurs. He means that it is a total absence, that it does not have any "positive content" which can be "pictured," that it is not a "state" in the sense described in the last paragraph. Let us call this the state or content-sense of "actuality" or "actuality$_s$." Now, Heidegger argues that since death is not an actuality in this latter sense, since it is not an actuality$_s$, it must therefore be a possibility. This conclusion would follow if it were true that whatever can be meaningfully talked about must either be an actuality$_s$ or a possibility; but this last proposition is an incomplete disjunction. It is most emphatically not true and we have just seen that it is not true. Death is not an actuality$_s$ and the same is true of our non-existence before birth. Death and non-existence before birth are neither actualities$_s$ nor possibilities. They are total absences. The statement that anything which is not an actuality$_s$ must be a possibility can only be rescued by a redefinition of "possibility" which in this instance is entirely arbitrary and perverse; and this is of course precisely what Heidegger has done.

It should be added that Heidegger is extremely unfair to those whom he describes as "brooding about" and to those who are said to "expect" death. I do not suppose that the "brooders" and the "expecters" are any more or less clear-headed in their thoughts about death than the rest of mankind (confining ourselves to all who do not seriously believe in survival). If so, then at times they probably vaguely think of death as a low-grade kind of consciousness; and to the extent to which they do this, they are in need of correction. However, at other times they realize only too well that death is a total absence and they presumably justify their gloom either because they have not enjoyed life and will, long before they would like this to happen, be deprived of any opportunities to make up for their previous lack of enjoyment, or because they have enjoyed and are enjoying life, but will, sooner or later, be utter "nullities" so that any continuation of their enjoyments will be impossible. When the brooders and the expecters regard death as an actuality, they almost certainly mean (most of the time at least) what is entirely true and what Heidegger does not dispute, namely, that they, like other human beings, will die, i.e., that their death will become an actuality$_o$.

Various of his disciples have claimed that Heidegger is to be credited with a major discovery in distinguishing "running ahead into the possibility" from mere "expecting." The realization that "vorlaufen" is "quite different" from mere "erwarten," Gelven tells us, fills "the mind with great enlightenment."[89] Schrag speaks of "vorlaufen" as the "activity" of "anticipatory appropriation" without which we cannot "authentically understand death."[90] In the course of this "anticipatory appropriation" death is "existentially preenacted."[91] Heideggerians like Gelvin and Schrag, whose minds are filled with "the great enlightenment" provided by Heidegger's notion of running ahead into the possibility, "existentially preenact" their death. Others less fortunate are condemned to an inauthentic life in which they merely expect death. It is suggested that it is possible to preenact death in a way that would correspond to our ability to *re*enact past events. However, since our anticipatory acts, whatever they may be, will always be "states" in the sense explained earlier and since death is a total absence, a preenactment of death is impossible. I can commit suicide or live dangerously, thereby courting an early death; but this would be "*en*actment" and not "preenactment" of death. I can start sleeping in a (suitably ventilated) coffin and I can simulate death; but none of this will be a "preenactment" of death analogous to the "reenactment" of past events. If "existential preenactment of death" is not to be a senseless expression, it can mean no more than realizing that one is going to die and that death is total annihilation and not a low-grade form of consciousness; and this is a feat which has been quite commonly accomplished without assistance from Heidegger.

I referred in passing to the fact that Sartre is one of those who has misunderstood what Heidegger means when he describes death as a possibility. Sartre thinks Heidegger is clearly wrong. Referring to death, he writes,

> this perpetual appearance of chance at the heart of my projects cannot be apprehended as *my* possibility but, on the contrary, as the nihilation of all my possibilities, a nihilation which *itself is no longer a part of my possibilities*. Thus death is not my possibility of no longer realizing a presence in the world but rather an *always possible nihilation of my possibles which is outside my possibilities*.[92]

Sartre is right to object to Heidegger, but he objects for the wrong reasons. When Heidegger finally explains what he means in this context by "possibility," it becomes clear that he is really saying just what Sartre is saying and what Russell is saying and what I am saying, namely, that death amounts to total extinction. Heidegger is *not wrong*, but *perverse*. He uses language which is almost certain to be misunderstood and the misuse, as I have indicated, is not completely unintentional.

6. *Living Dying and Dead Dying*

It should be noted that Heideggerians constantly do precisely what is impermissible if we are to be guided by Heidegger's explanation of what he opposes in calling death a possibility. They constantly "reify" death, i.e., they regard it as an "actuality" in the objectionable sense of the term. We already saw how Father Demske's enthusiasm led him to the remarkable conclusion that death is the crown and culmination of human life and how Wild and Schrag came to speak of it as a task and act. Similar reifications, but not so explicitly, are indulged in by numerous Heideggerians and by Heidegger himself when they point to the "methodological difficulties" which one encounters in dealing with the question "what is death?" Father Boros has been much concerned with these problems. "Philosophical reflections on death," he observes, "seem to have no point since we have no direct experience of death."[93] Perhaps, Boros suggests, we can get around this difficulty by watching other people die. Unfortunately this will not solve the problem. For "as we watch at somebody's death-bed" what we witness "is assuredly not death *in its inner reality*; it is only the outward aspect of death."[94] Boros then inquires whether we might not "receive a decisive, revealing answer from people who have been near death, or have been given up for dead by those about them." Such an inquiry, alas, will also fail to answer our questions since people who were close to death did not really experience *death* as distinct from *closeness* to death.

Macquarrie has gone into great detail about these seemingly insuperable difficulties. In an essay entitled "Death and Its Significance," in which he commends Heidegger's teachings to his fellow-Christians as "a sound and contemporary basis on which to rear" their "theological superstructure,"[95] Macquarrie is concerned to explore what he calls the "ontological" or "existential" character of death. How, he asks, can a person "understand" his "own death"? Macquarrie has been greatly impressed by the "phenomenological method" as employed by Heidegger in his "existential analytic." By using this method Heidegger has succeeded in throwing much light on such "structures" as "understanding, moods, speech, anxiety, concern and solicitude." These structures can be phenomenologically explored in our living through them, but our death is something "which we do *not* live through."[96] If so, how can death be "investigated phenomenologically" and, what is apparently the same thing, how could we achieve an "existential understanding" of death? The situation of the ontological explorer seems quite desperate:

> Anyone who undergoes death seems by that very fact to be robbed of any possibility of understanding and analyzing what it was to undergo death. He has ceased to be, therefore he has ceased to be disclosed to himself; his being is no longer lit up to himself in the only way that would seem to make anything like an existential analysis possible, and so it appears that he cannot by any means understand what the undergoing of death may be like, as an existential phenomenon.[97]

In another work Macquarrie has succinctly described the plight of the phenomenological investigator who has died:

> He has ceased to be . . . Therefore he has ceased to be disclosed to himself, and has no possibility of understanding what his death has been.[98]

In his despair, Macquarrie, like Boros, raises the question whether relevant "information may be obtained" by studying the death of other people. At first sight this appears a promising possibility. For, in the case of other people who die before we do, we "can see them ceasing to exist, going out of the world, so to speak."[99] Further reflection, however, shows that studying the death of others will not get us out of our predicament. There are two devastating objections to anybody who thinks otherwise. In the first place, such a study yields no more than "a vicarious experience of death." When we study the death of others what we are experiencing is the loss sustained by the survivors, "but what is really of interest to us is the *loss of being sustained by the deceased himself,* and this remains completely inaccessible to us."[100] Moreover, as already observed, the deceased, being deceased, cannot attend to his deadness—he cannot experience his loss of being; and, even if he could, he would be unable to tell the living what this loss of being is like. He can no "longer communicate with us to describe that loss of being."[101]

Boros and Macquarrie have in effect reified death in exactly the way Heidegger regards as impermissible when he (unfairly) denounces the brooders and expecters and when he tells us that death is not an actuality. The "inner reality" of the dead person's death and the "loss of being sustained by the deceased himself" which he finds it impossible to describe to us, are treated as dark and mysterious states whose nature we would like to discover but which, for the reasons indicated, we find it extremely difficult to explore. This "inquiry," it must now be added, is by no means an accidental aberration on the part of two Heideggerian enthusiasts. It is found in many other Heideggerians and in Heidegger himself.[102] We would like to "grasp," writes

Heidegger, "the way-to-be" referred to as "coming-to-an-end." We are "asking about the ontological meaning of the dying of the person who dies." (BT, p. 283) Just like Boros and Macquarrie, Heidegger first points out that nobody can experience his own death:

> When Dasein reaches its wholeness in death, it simultaneously loses the Being of its "there." By its transition to no-longer-Dasein, it gets lifted right out of the possibility of experiencing this transition and of understanding it as something experienced. Surely this sort of thing is denied to any particular Dasein in relation to itself. (BT, p. 281)

Heidegger then turns to the question of the death of other people and, like Boros and Macquarrie, he concludes that it is of no help to us:

> In such Being-with-the-dead, the authentic Being-come-to-an-end of the deceased is precisely the sort of thing which we do *not* experience. Death does indeed reveal itself as a loss, but a loss such as is experienced by those who remain. In suffering this loss, however, we have no way of access to the loss-of-Being as such which the dying man "suffers." (p. 282, Heidegger's italics)

Again, in a later section, we are told that

> a psychology of "dying" gives information about the "living" of the person who is "dying" rather than about *dying itself*. (p. 291, my italics)

In other words, there are two kinds of "dying." There is the "dying" a person experiences before he is dead, what is *usually* called "dying" and this "living dying" we *can* study; but there is also the "dying itself," the dying that occurs after the person is dead, his "dead dying," which is identical with what I above called deadness. The "dead or non-living dying" is the loss of being sustained by the deceased; and *its* nature will not be revealed in our study of the "living dying" of others. Thus, although Heidegger (rightly in my opinion) insists with great emphasis that death is a total absence and not an actuality$_s$, he also, quite inconsistently, treats death as such an actuality.

It may be noted in passing that Boros, Macquarrie and Heidegger himself believe that, in spite of their extreme gravity, the methodological problems resulting from our inability to attend to our own deadness can be overcome. "Modern philosophy has gone far," writes Father Boros, toward overcoming these difficulties. It will come as no surprise that the "modern philosophy" referred to by Boros is that expounded by Martin Heidegger in *BT*. This philosophy has shown that "in every act of existence death is present from the beginning."[103] Similarly, Macquarrie observes that "existence is dying, and death is present to us."[104] Since it is "in a sense already in the present," it is after all "accessible . . . to the investigation of the existential analytic."[105] If we recall the distinction explained in Section 3 between d_o—death in the ordinary sense—and c_d—our concern about death—it will at once be obvious that "modern philosophy" has not overcome the methodological difficulties which so greatly perplexed the phenomenological explorers. For what we experience, what is available for phenomenological analysis, what becomes "transparent" is not death, d_o, but c_d or thoughts and moods concerning death; and these were always available, even before Heidegger's "existential" analysis. What was not available for phenomenological exploration prior to Heidegger's interiorization is just as unavailable afterwards.

It is hardly necessary to add that the methodological difficulties themselves are completely spurious. If one first misconceives death as the "inner state" of the dead person whose dead body is "the outward aspect" of his death or as the state in which the dead person has sustained the most terrible of all losses, then one is bound to be mystified. One will conclude that such a state is inaccessible to the outside observer who only perceives the "living dying" and "the outward aspect"; and it is of course equally inaccessible to the dead person who, being dead, is unable to attend to his deadness. However, there is no justification for thinking about death in this way. If, in agreement with the Heidegger who speaks of death as an utter nullity, we regard it as simply the total absence of experiences and behavior, the "methodological difficulties" instantly disappear. My deadness after I have died is no more incomprehensible to me than the fact that I did not exist before I was born or, if you like, before I was conceived. I understand perfectly well what is meant by the statement that I was not yet alive in 1800 although I was not then around to do any phenomenological exploring. Similarly, I do not have to be dead and, as a dead man, engage in phenomenological investigations in order to understand *now*, while I am alive, that I will be dead in the year 2100.

7.   *Double-Talk about Survival after Death*

Bertrand Russell makes Heidegger's point about the totality of the destruction which death involves not only more simply and clearly, but also without any equivocation on the subject of survival. The reader will be surprised to hear that, in spite of his completely unqualified assertion that death is "the impossibility of every way of comporting oneself towards anything, of every way of existing" and his equally unqualified characterization of death as a total nullity, Heidegger also claims that his analysis leaves the question of survival entirely open. His "this-worldly ontological Interpretation of death," Heidegger says, "takes precedence over any ontical other-worldly speculation" but he does not at all rule out such speculation. His investigation

does not imply any ontical decision whether "after death" still another Being is possible, either higher or lower, or whether Dasein "lives on" or even "outlasts" itself and is "immortal." Nor is anything decided ontically about the "other-worldly" and its possibility, any more than about the "this-worldly." (p. 292)[106]

Heidegger's followers seem entirely satisfied that there is no incompatibility between these two sets of statements. "Heidegger's ontological analysis," writes Schrag approvingly,

> remains intentionally neutral to the material content of any special ontic inter-pretation of death. He has sought to clarify the ontological-existentialist founda-tion which is presupposed by any ontic-existential understanding, but he has not taken into his program the task of elucidating death in connection with its biological, psychological, or theological significance.[107]

"The question," furthermore,

> of man having some kind of "being" after death is left open . . . Heidegger's inter-pretation of man, as ontology, remains indifferent to any material content which may be supplied by a religious world-view or theological conviction.[108]

In much the same way Alwin Diemer maintains that Heidegger's conclusions about death do not "in the least" amount to a "denial of the immortality of men." Those who attribute such a position to Heidegger "confuse ontological and ontic problems."[109] Unlike Heidegger, Schrag proceeds to inform us how the ontic question of survival *is* to be resolved. "There," he writes, "man's concrete ethical and religious experience must constitute the court of final appeal."[110] Schrag in one place discusses suicide and I believe he would claim his conclusion to be entirely consistent with Heidegger's teachings about death. Suicide, he tells us,

> provides no exit—neither the suicide in which the self succumbs to weakness nor the suicide of a defiant self-affirmation. Suicide solves only the problem of bodily annihilation, but the self is not exhausted in its mode as a living body.[111]

I confess I find all of this extremely puzzling. If death is really "the im-possibility of *every* way of comporting oneself towards anything and of *every* way of existing," if it is an utter nullity then we do not survive. Conversely, if the question of survival is left open, then we have no right to declare, flatly, as something true without qualification, that death is an utter nullity. I do not know anything that could be plainer than this. The statement that "on-tologically" death is indeed total annihilation, but that "ontically" we may nevertheless survive, shows only one thing, namely, that much of the time the distinction between "ontological" and "ontic" questions is exceedingly nebulous. One is reminded of the medieval doctrine of the "two-fold truth," according to which a proposition may be false as a matter of reason but nevertheless true as a matter of faith. If, "ontologically," death is total an-nihilation, this is presumably a true statement; and if it is a true statement, in what sense could it also not be true? Moreover, all of Heidegger's talk about anxiety (as contrasted with fear) to which we shall turn in the next section, as well as his numerous comments about the flight from this anxiety on the part of everyday Dasein make no sense unless death is really total annihilation.

Although the distinction between "ontological" and "ontic" is never clearly explained, either by Heidegger or by any of his followers, one does in *certain contexts* get a reasonably good idea of what is intended. An "ontological" characteristic of human beings appears to be one which is essentially connected with their humanity; and "ontic" characteristic is one that is not so connected. My concern for the future, my "running ahead" of myself, for example, would be an ontological characteristic because it is essentially connected with my humanity; and the same would apply to the fact that I can and must make choices. The fact that I weigh 150 pounds or that I like steak but don't like fish are ontic characteristics since I would or could be a human being even if my weight and tastes were different. The same is true of *specific* choices I make. That I can and must make choices is an ontological feature, but that I choose this rather than that is an ontic fact. Heideggerians usually explain the distinction by saying that ontological discourse is concerned with Being while ontic statements refer to things or beings. Ontology for Heidegger, in the words of Herbert Spiegelberg, one of the most reliable and sober expositors of the theories of phenomenologists and existentialists, is "the study of Being as opposed to that of the things-in-being."[112] "Ontological inquiry," Heidegger himself writes, "is more primordial, as over against the ontical inquiry of the positive sciences." (BT, p. 31) M-R, in a footnote, point out that Heidegger does not explicitly define the words "ontological" and "ontical," but they add that "their meanings will emerge rather clearly." They then add their own explanations: "Ontological inquiry is concerned primarily with *Being*; ontical inquiry is concerned primarily with entities and the facts about them." (M-R's italics) "For Heidegger," writes Webster F. Hood, "to conceive something in its ontic dimension means that one grasps how it is related to other entities; but to conceive something in its ontological dimension to to appreciate how it is related to Being, to appreciate exactly how Being makes this entity possible."[113] Demske, who defines ontology as "the science of being," explains that "ontological" refers to "the deeper level of intelligibility, the realm of the underlying structures," while "ontic" refers to "the more immediate surface level of the concrete acts of existence." "Ontological," again, refers to "the internal structures which underly and constitute the being of a being as its conditions of possibility." "Ontic," on the other hand, refers to "those actions which are externally observable, which are made possible by ontological structures."[114] Since the word "Being" is notoriously obscure, these definitions are not very helpful. William Barrett speaks of Being as "the unutterable"[115] and Heidegger himself has spoken of it as the "das Ungreifbare" ("the ungraspable"), "das Unbestimmte, Unbestimmbare" ("that which cannot be specified," "the indefinable"), "das Unumgängliche" ("that which cannot be covered or sur-rounded"), and "das sich verbergende Einzige" ("the unique which conceals itself").[116] Richard Schmitt, a critical and very able commentator, argues that "the distinction between ontic and ontological talk closely parallels the familiar distinction that is often referred to by contrasting factual statements with statements about categories," admitting that the latter is not itself a clear distinction.[117] I do not see that any of these interpretations, even allowing them to be coherent, avoid the inconsistency I have mentioned. Con-fining myself to Father Demske's formulation, it seems quite absurd to main-tain *both* that on the "deeper level of intelligibility" death amounts to total annihilation *and* that on "the more immediate surface level of life" which is "externally observable" human beings may nevertheless live forever.

Schrag's statement that "suicide provides no exit" is equally inconsistent with Heidegger's "ontological" analysis. The late Percy Bridgman was not only a distinguished physicist, but also a man of great courage and integrity. When he found that he was suffering from incurable cancer he shot himself. If Heidegger is right in regarding death as total annihilation, then Professor Bridgman's suicide *did* provide an exit—he saved himself what he regarded as pointless misery and pain. The self may not be "exhausted in its mode as a living body," but if death is "the impossibility of *every* way of existing," then any of the self's modes other than "its mode as a living body" would also be annihilated. As for Schrag's claim that "ethical and religious experience con-stitute the court of final appeal" in settling such questions as that of survival, it should be remarked that it involves a confusion between causal or genetic questions and questions of justification. Powerful religious experiences or ethical demands may *cause* a man to believe in survival. This does not mean that they *justify* such a belief, i.e., that they are any kind of evidence for it. It is far from clear, for example, how ethical or religious experiences could cancel out the overwhelming evidence we have that human consciousness is causally dependent on the brain and nervous system.[118]

Much the same inconsistency, sometimes in an even more flagrant form, without the ontological-ontic distinction as camouflage, is found in almost every other Heideggerian who has written on this topic. This is particularly true of Peter Koestenbaum who may be described as a Heideggerian writing for the masses. In an article suitably entitled "The Vitality of Death" which was recently reprinted in a book bearing the same title, he shows himself deeply imbued with Heidegger's teachings. In a striking passage Koesten-baum observes that "the most vitalizing fact of life is the utter inevitability of death," something which a human being "must constantly keep before his eyes."[119] The realization that death is the end "leads automatically to what in the business world is called 'thinking big'."[120] Exactly the same position is advocated in an introductory textbook in which Koestenbaum addresses himself to problems about the meaning of life. The last chapter is entitled

"The Philosophy of Existentialism" and in it he develops the implications of Heidegger's "famous existential analysis of man with reference to the first-person experiences of time, death, guilt, and authenticity." The "full recognition of man's finitude," as it is taught by Heidegger and other existentialists,

> is the sole thing that gives man the courage to take the bull of his life by the horns and subdue it into a meaningful existence.[121]

A little later he turns to a discussion of the anxiety induced by the realization of the finality of death:

> My life has meaning, that is, authenticity, only to the extent that I face clearly the certainty of my own death. I am an authentic *man* only to the extent that I accept unequivocally the ever-present anxiety about my non-being. The threat of my eventual and *total extinction* is and should be the single most pervasive fact of my human life and my human existence.[122]

However, in *Managing Anxiety*, a self-help book in which, among many other things, Koestenbaum applies Heideggerian ideas to problems of the nursing profession, he actively supports belief in immortality. The last chapter of this book deals with "the existential meaning of death" and the problems of a "public health nurse." He begins by telling the nurse that in order to help dying patients, she must herself "be ready to die today."[123] Koestenbaum does not inform us whether he actually gave this advice to any nurses or, if he did, how they responded. So far as I know, Koestenbaum has not worked with dying patients, but he has not the slightest doubt that if such a patient can be convinced of "the indestructibility of consciousness," either as the result of "philosophical analysis" or by means of "religious metaphor," he will face his death with joy:

> He experiences the peace of one who knows that he is an indestructible consciousness not necessarily involved with the world. The dying person who is reconciled in this fashion has become in effect the saintly ascetic revered by all the world cultures in all periods of history. He participates in his death.[124]

Koestenbaum then addresses the nurse and asks her whether she can accept the belief in personal immortality "theoretically, practically and feelingly." "If you are to be fully effective," he tells her, "your answer has to be 'yes'."[125] Nurses who do not accept the belief in personal immortality "theoretically, practically and feelingly" would be well advised to turn to another of Koestenbaum's efforts entitled *Is There an Answer to Death?* In it they will find not only a highly original argument proving conclusively—at least to Koestenbaum's satisfaction—the indestructibility of consciousness, but also a set of "Immortality Excercises" in the course of which they can literally experience their own eternity.[126] One wonders what has happened to the notion that death is "total extinction" which in the first place made

Koestenbaum "think big" and "take the bull of his life by the horns and sub-
due it into a meaningful existence"?

I suspect that most Heideggerians, while endorsing Koestenbaum's advice to nurses, would disavow his invention of "Immortality Excercises" as
well as some of his other more bizarre concoctions. In "The Vitality of
Death" Koestenbaum reaches the frightening conclusion that when he dies
the world will cease to exist. I think that Heideggerians will join the rest of us
in hoping that in this connection Koestenbaum over-estimated the impor-
tance of his place in the scheme of things. However, in spite of these
differences, many of the more sedate Heideggerians teach, just like Koestenbaum, that death means total destruction and that nevertheless human beings
are immortal. Glenn Gray, for example, whose credentials as a Heideggerian
are unimpeachable and who addresses himself not to nurses and psychiatric
patients but to a philosophical audience, first refers to the "existential dread"
which grips us when we contemplate "the prospect of no longer being, of
vanishing into nullity."[127] "The positivist," we are assured in this connection,
"has no weapon against this dread, this shudder at Non-being."[128] The
Heideggerian, it appears, who has achieved "genuine personality" and
therefore "resoluteness" does have a weapon against this dread. "He will no
longer avoid exposure nor the shudder of dread before Nothingness. On the
contrary these will be his meat and drink."[129] Whatever one may think of
these "weapons," it seems clear that the "authentic" individual who has
achieved "genuine personality" will truthfully regard death as a "nullity,"
i.e., as total annihilation. When we get to the end of the same essay, however,
we find that the genuine personality is nevertheless entitled to faith in a
hereafter. We are told that "there must be some deep-seated faith that we are
not suspended over an abyss." Although we may have a yearning for
rationality, this yearning "must make place for religious faith and larger
meanings." We "need not renounce our conviction that death as an occurrence holds, also, the promise of a greater fullness of Being."[130] I should
perhaps add that I am endlessly astonished that many Christians, Catholics
as well as Protestants, are followers of Heidegger and have expressed their
total acceptance of his teachings on death. They appear to see no inconsistency in accepting Heidegger's view that death is a "total nullity" and their
Christian faith in eternal life after death. Thus, John Macquarrie, who is a
leading Protestant theologian, in the very same book[131] in which he defends
Heidegger's views on death, also has extensive discussions of eschatology in
an entirely affirmative spirit, implying that Christian statements about the
eternal life awaiting us after death are perfectly correct. I hope that one of
these days a Christian follower of Heidegger will explain how it is possible to
maintain *both* that death means total annihilation *and* that in spite of this
total annihilation we shall live forever.[132]

8. Death, Anxiety and the Nothing

That Dasein "has been delivered over to its death," Heidegger tells us, is not something of which we have "for the most part . . . explicit or even any theoretical knowledge." (p. 295) Our "thrownness into death reveals itself . . . in a more primordial and impressive manner in . . . anxiety" (*Ibid.*). "Being-towards-death," in fact, "is essentially anxiety" (p. 310). It is essentially "anxiety" but not "fear"; and Heidegger is very concerned to distinguish "anxiety in the face of death" from "fear in the face of one's demise" (p. 295).[133] The distinction, it appears, is between concern about what we earlier called deadness and fear of what we called the death-producing event.

Anxiety, in the face of death, is "not an accidental or random mood of 'weakness' in some individual" (p. 295). On the contrary, it is "a basic state-of-mind of Dasein" (*Ibid.*) and, as Heidegger elsewhere assures us, fear itself is only possible because "anxiety is always latent" (p. 234). In fact "fear is anxiety, fallen into the 'world', inauthentic, and as such, hidden from itself" (*Ibid.*). The villain in our story, as is usual in Heidegger, is the "they":

> The "they" concerns itself with transforming this anxiety into fear in the face of an oncoming event. In addition, the anxiety which has been made ambiguous as fear, is passed off as a weakness with which no self-assured Dasein may have any acquaintance. What is "fitting" according to the unuttered decree of the "they," is indifferent tranquillity as to the "fact" that one dies. (p. 298)

The "they," furthermore, denounces "thinking about death" as "a cowardly fear, a sign of insecurity on the part of Dasein, and a somber way of fleeing from the world" (*Ibid.*). According to Heidegger, the reverse is true. It is fear and not anxiety which is "cowardly." Inauthentic Dasein "perverts anxiety into cowardly fear and, in surmounting this fear, only makes known its own cowardliness in the face of anxiety" (p. 311). Moreover, it is true that anxiety tears Dasein away from the world, but this is all to the good. Dasein then can no longer "understand itself . . . in terms of 'the world' and the way things have been publicly interpreted" (p. 232). In this way Dasein is "thrown back" upon itself and can achieve authenticity.

Anxiety, as we have seen, is the mood or state of mind which gives us our "primordial" and non-theoretical knowledge that we must die. According to Heidegger, it plays another extremely important role in our proper understanding of death. Heidegger repeatedly emphasizes that, although death is certain, its timing is uncertain. We know that we will die but we do not know when our death will occur:

> Running ahead brings Dasein face-to-face with a possibility which is constantly certain but which at any moment remains indefinite as to when that possibility will become an impossibility. (p. 356, G. 308)

It scarcely needs to be mentioned that the "they" once again appears on the scene to do its nefarious work. "The 'they'," we are told, "covers up what is peculiar in death's certainty—*that it is possible at any moment*" (p. 302, Heidegger's italics). The "they" evades "the indefiniteness by conferring definiteness upon it" (*Ibid.*) The "they" goes about this cover up in an extremely clever way. It does not "confer definiteness" upon death by trying to calculate the date of the demise. This kind of definiteness would frighten an inauthentic Dasein too much. It therefore defers death to "sometime later" and "interposes" before death

> those urgencies and possibilities which can be taken in at a glance, and which belong to the everyday matters that are closest to us. (p. 302)

Once we have chased away the "they," we are faced with a serious "existential" problem. "Can Dasein," Heidegger asks, ". . . *understand authentically* its ownmost possibility . . . which is certain and, as such, indefinite?" (p. 304, Heidegger's italics). More specifically: how does "running ahead" which discloses the indefiniteness of death accomplish this disclosure?

> How does the running ahead understanding project itself upon a potentiality-for-Being which is certain and which is constantly possible in such a way that the "when" in which the utter impossibility of existence becomes possible remains constantly indefinite? (p. 310, G 265)

This is not, Heidegger implies, an idle or trivial question. Quite the reverse:

> In running ahead into the indefinite certainty of death, Dasein opens itself ("öffnet sich") to a *constant threat* arising out of its own "there." (*Ibid.*, Heidegger's italics)

This "opening" is an essential part of "authentic Being-towards-death."

> In this very threat Being-towards-the-end must maintain itself. So little can it tone this down that it must rather cultivate the indefiniteness of the certainty. (*Ibid.*)

But how can this be done? This "openness" in which we "must maintain" ourselves and which we "must cultivate" is something more than a mere theoretical understanding of the fact that the timing of our death is uncertain. "How," asks Heidegger, "is it existentially possible for this constant threat to be genuinely disclosed?" All understanding, he has repeatedly asserted, is accompanied by a mood or state-of-mind. What is the state-of-mind which "genuinely discloses" not just that we must die but that the certainty of death is indefinite? Once again anxiety fills the breach. "The indefiniteness of death is primordially disclosed in anxiety" (p. 356). Again: "*The state-of-mind which can hold open the utter and constant threat to itself . . . is anxiety*" (p. 310, Heidegger's italics).

It thus appears that two doses of anxiety are in store for an authentic Dasein. It experiences anxiety both when it is face-to-face with its deadness and when it contemplates the indefiniteness of the time of its demise. The latter presumably serves to intensify the anxiety already experienced by the mere contemplation of deadness. Heidegger clearly implies that the greater the anxiety, the more desirable is the experience. It is only in this way that we can explain his recommendation that Dasein should "cultivate the indefiniteness of the certainty." This view has not only appealed to Heidegger's disciples. Wolfgang Stegmüller, a German analytic philosopher who is highly critical of certain aspects of Heidegger's thought, nevertheless finds in his work "a virtually inexhaustible abundance of new . . . insights."[134] One of these, it appears, is the recommendation just mentioned:

> Authentic Being-towards-death can consist only in the fact that death is not evaded but endured, and indeed precisely in its character as an indeterminate possibility. Such enduring is for Heidegger the ultimate ideal of Existence . . . Here Dasein first reaches its supreme authenticity.[135]

All of this is reminiscent of Kierkegaard's teaching that "passion"—not just any passion but "the tension of inwardness" produced in the person who has faith in the existence of God and the divinity of Jesus in spite of the logical difficulties involved in such beliefs—"is the culmination of existence for an existing individual."[136]

Before continuing with the account of what Heidegger means by "anxiety" a further explanation is required of his view on the nature of fear. According to Heidegger fear always has a definite "wovor" ("that before which one is or stands"). When we experience fear, we are "in the face of a detrimental entity within-the-world which comes from some definite region" (p. 230). We are then "always afraid of this or that definite thing which threatens us in this or that definite way."[137] If a person has been sentenced to death, what we would, in everyday language, call his "fear" of the execution would also be called "fear" by Heidegger. It has an object or a "wovor." Does anxiety have an object? The answer is "yes and no." It does not have an object in the sense of being directed to some particular "detrimental entity within the world." However, if saying that it has an object means no more than that it has a direction, then anxiety does have an object. Heidegger offers various accounts of the nature of this object and this direction. In Section 40 of *BT* he tells us several times that the "wovor" of anxiety is *"the world as such"* (p. 231, Heidegger's italics) or *"being-in-the-world-itself"* (p. 232, Heidegger's italics). In the same section he writes that "in anxiety what is environmentally ready-to-hand sinks away and, so in general, do entities within-the-world." When all these entities "sink away," "the 'world' can offer nothing more, and neither can the Dasein-with of others" (p. 232). Saying that we are anxious in the face of the world as such, he tells us, is equivalent to the statement that we are anxious of the Nothing (p. 232, G. 187). I do not profess to understand all of this, but talk about "the Nothing" as the "wovor" of anxiety becomes much clearer when Heidegger discusses anxiety in connection with death. In a passage which I quoted in a previous section (p. 354, G. 306) Heidegger tells us that, "the impossibility of existence" which death is seen to be is "die schlechthinnige Nichtigkeit des Daseins"—"the utter nothingness (nullity) of Dasein." It is utter nothingness which Dasein must face in anxiety. "In this state-of-mind, Dasein finds itself *face-to-face* with the Nothing of the possible impossibility of its existence" (p. 310, G. 266). Again:

> The Nothing with which anxiety brings us face-to-face, unveils the nothingness by which Dasein, in its very *basis* is defined; and this basis itself is thrownness into death.[138] (p. 356, G. 308, Heidegger's italics)

The nature of this Nothing is further explored in "Was ist Metaphysik?", in the first of the lectures which make up *Introduction to Metaphysics*, and in several later writings. The Nothing is not a being or an object ("Gegenstand"). Nevertheless it is in some important sense real and the fact that science does not recognize it only shows the narrowness of science:

> It is perfectly true that one cannot talk or deliberate about the Nothing, as though it were a thing like the rain outside or the mountain or any object whatsoever. The Nothing remains in principle inaccessible to science. A person who really wants to talk about the Nothing must become unscientific.[139]

It must be remembered that no "strictness of a science reaches the seriousness of metaphysics" and that "philosophy can never be judged by the standards of science."[140] In fact, for reasons we shall not go into here, Heidegger maintains that science itself is possible only because man "projects himself into the Nothing."[141] In Volume 2 of his *Nietzsche* Heidegger denounces with great vehemence the philosophers who make fun of his talk about the Nothing as an "empty play with words." The so-called "reflections" of these people are impressive only as long as we "move in the region of what is easily intelligible." His opponents are guilty of gross "thoughtlessness" and, in contrast to Heidegger himself, "operate with mere words." Although it is not easy to talk about it without appearing to involve oneself in contradiction, the Nothing is very real and "need not be sought or found" if only because it is "what we can never lose."[142]

The Nothing is not only in some sense real, but it also engages in an activity or a quasi-activity to which Heidegger refers as "nichten" and which is variously translated as "nihilating" or "nothinging." The Nothing is "essentially repulsing" (or "repelling"—the German is "wesenhaft abweisend"). This "nothinging" or "repulsing" is not the same thing as annihilation ("Vernichtung"); and it also is not identical with negation ("Verneinung")

although negation is not unrelated to the nothinging of the Nothing. Originally, the Nothing is present as a datum[143] only in anxiety, but much else
"testifies" to its "constant although admittedly veiled presence."[144] Negation
as a logical operation "is grounded in the Nothing, i.e., it originates from the
nothinging of the Nothing." In a passage which has frequently been quoted
Heidegger asks:

> Is the Nothing real only because of the existence of the not, i.e., of negation? Or is
> it the other way around: do negation and the not exist only because of the reality
> of the Nothing?[145]

In opposition to the "dominant and unquestioned teaching of 'logic' "
Heidegger replies that "the Nothing is more original than the not and
negation."[146] Negation is only one and "by no means the leading" mode of
conduct that is grounded in the nothinging of the Nothing.[147] There are
various other situations in which Dasein is "thoroughly shaken"
("durchschüttert") by the nothinging of the Nothing:

> Deeper than . . . mere rational negation is the harshness of opposition and the
> pungency of loathing. More responsible [than mere rational negation] is the pain
> of failure and the mercilessness of a prohibition, more burdensome the bitterness
> of renunciation.[148]

Heidegger's view that, in the course of anxiety in the face of death, we
experience the Nothing is endorsed not only by out-and-out Heideggerians,
but also by many more independent existentialists. They all believe that in
some sense the Nothing or Non-Being is real—in a sense in which this is not
allowed by positivists and most ordinary people—and that our most obvious
(although not our only) encounter with the Nothing occurs in the course of
our thoughts and feelings about death. Thus, Tillich, who like Heidegger
believes that we cannot account for the existence of negative judgments
without postulating the reality of "non-being" (his word corresponding to
Heidegger's "the Nothing"), also maintains that we directly experience this
non-being in the course of two "shocks." One of these "shocks" is experienced by "those who are philosophers by nature" when they realize in their
"theoretic imagination" that, although there *are* things, there might have
been nothing. The other shock of non-being is one that can also be experienced by "a simple human being." He experiences it in "the practical experience
of having to die."[149] Similarly, Macquarrie, who concedes that philosophers
like Carnap "have some excellent sport in shooting down the kind of talk
[about the Nothing] which we meet in Heidegger and others" and who
presumably agrees that Heidegger is mistaken in regarding "nothing," in its
ordinary sense, as a name, insists that Heidegger is not talking nonsense.
Heidegger is not talking nonsense because "nothing," as it is used by him,
does have "something like an empirical anchor."[150] In the "existential

situation" with which Heidegger is concerned, talk about the Nothing "not only makes sense but very good sense indeed."[151] The "existential situation" which gives content to Heidegger's use of "nothing" is "the mood of anxiety" which "discloses" to us "the possibility of ceasing to be." " 'Nothing' stands for the disclosure in our experience as existents of this possibility of ceasing to be."[152] Again:

> Anxiety makes manifest the nullity . . . that enters into the very constitution of man's being . . . Anxiety in the face of death . . . brings man to confront nothing.[153]

There is a great deal in the various statements by Heidegger and the other writers I have quoted which is in one way or another open to question. Among many other things, I find Heidegger's strictures on the "they" in connection with its alleged "veiling" of the indefiniteness of death totally absurd. It is true that death is "possible at any moment," but, unless we have strong reason to expect its occurrence in the immediate or very near future, it is just elementary good sense to treat it as something that will happen "sometime later" (which—contrary to Heidegger's assertion—is not making it definite) and to get on with whatever "urgency" may be at hand. The moment we bring the Heidegger-Stegmüller talk about "enduring death as an indeterminate possibility" down to earth, it is seen to be empty and grotesque posturing. If a surgeon is about to operate to restore a person's health, should he not proceed with this "urgency" in order to endure the indefiniteness of his death? If a singer is about to give a recital should he cancel it so that he can instead cultivate the anxiety with which Heidegger wants us to contemplate the uncertain "when" of his death? Should a person who is not very old and who is in good health not set out on a major project like a scientific investigation or the composition of a symphony just because he *may* die at any moment? If none of these suggestions are implied in Heidegger's recommendation, just what *is* its content? Turning to Heidegger's talk about the Nothing, the first and perhaps most obvious criticism is that he seems quite unable to provide a proper statement of what is at issue between him and those whom he calls the defenders of logic. According to Heidegger's formulation both of the opposing positions accept the reality of the Nothing and the only question is whether the Nothing is more "original" than negation. The fact is of course that Heidegger's opponents do *not* allow the reality of his Nothing: they maintain that in order to give an adequate account of the nature of negative judgments, we do not need to introduce such a weird referent at all. Again, nobody with the slightest intellectual honesty can be satisfied that Heidegger has adequately explained what he means by "nichten," the "nothinging" in which the Nothing is supposedly engaged. However, I do not intend to pursue these and other pertinent objections here. I will confine myself to a discussion of two of Heidegger's claims, (1) that to give an adequate account of human moods, especially as they relate to death, we must include anxiety (in his special sense) as well as fear and (2) that if one admits the reality of anxiety as a special mood one is thereby committed to accepting the reality of his Nothing. I shall give reasons for accepting (1) and for rejecting (2). More specifically, I shall try to show that Heidegger calls attention to something of interest in distinguishing anxiety, at least as it relates to death, from other members of the fear-family. His formulations are oracular and exceedingly cryptic, but a sympathetic reading will show that he has a substantive point which can be stated simply and clearly. I will also try to show that admission of the facts about anxiety to which Heidegger calls attention does not imply any of his claims about the reality of the Nothing. Since a great many confusions surround the entire subject of absences and nothingness, even in the writings of philosophers who have no connection with existentialism, I will also offer a few clarifying comments of a more general nature.

I will begin by pointing out that in a certain quite straight-forward sense absences are just as real as presences. Some years ago I entertained a distinguished acquaintance at an expensive restaurant. I intended to express my appreciation of many kindnesses he had shown me over a number of years. When the bill came I discovered to my great embarrassment that I had no money in my pocket. The absence of money was just as much a fact as the presence of money is a fact on other occasions. If I look in the refrigerator for oranges and find no other fruit than an apple and some peaches I thereby discover the absence of oranges. The absence of oranges is just as real, just as indisputable a fact as the presence of the apple and the peaches. Just like presences, absences can be frightening, embarrassing, tragic and also delightful. The absence of the eyes of a person who has become blind is a tragic absence. The absence of money can be highly embarrassing. The absence of a hated tyrant, whether he is a political leader or the chairman of a department or the foreman in a factory, will be exhilarating. The presence of an illness can be depressing and upsetting. The absence of the same illness, after it has been cured, can be a source of delight.

My statement that absences are real must not be misconstrued as committing me to various metaphysical theories that some readers, especially existentialists, are liable to read into it. In the first place I am not asserting the existence or reality of "non-things," a weird species of entity exemplified by non-oranges, non-money, non-cancer, etc. Admitting that there are true negative statements no more requires one to postulate such non-things than admitting that there are true disjunctions requires one to postulate "disjunctive entities." A naturalist examining footprints may be in a position to assert quite correctly, "these are the footprints of a tiger or a lion." To account for the truth of this statement it is not necessary to introduce an animal or quasi-animal called "lion or tiger" in addition to tigers and lions. Similarly, the truth of the statement "there are no oranges in the refrigerator" does not presuppose that there are entities called "non-oranges." In saying that absences are real I am also not saying that the absence of absent things is one of their characteristics. The absence of absent oranges is not a characteristic of oranges the way sweetness or roundness may be characteristics of oranges. Finally, I am not saying that there are "negative facts" except in the innocuous sense in which this is another way of saying that there are true negative statements. I am *not* saying that there are negative facts in a sense in which this is a metaphysical thesis that has been advocated by many philosophers, for example, by Bertrand Russell in his lectures on "The Philosophy of Logical Atomism."[154] My objection to this thesis is not primarily to its postulation of *negative* facts but to its postulation of *facts* as part of the "furniture of the world." There are things which have qualities and stand in certain relations to one another and we make true and false statements; but there is no reason for adding a further kind of entity, called "facts," positive or negative. There are sweet red apples in the refrigerator, but there is not a further entity called "the fact that there are sweet red apples in the refrigerator." The expression "it is a fact that" is not of course meaningless, but it is just another way of asserting a given statement.[155]

The admission of the reality of absences in the sense explained in no way commits one to accepting Heidegger's various statements about the Nothing. This can be shown independently of deciding whether Heidegger is talking sense in this connection or what the sense of his statements is, if they have any. It can be shown as the result of his quite explicit declaration that the Nothing cannot be discovered by ordinary observation, that it is a reality which falls outside the domain of scientific investigation. Quite clearly, absences are ascertained by the same ordinary observations as presences. No special "existential mood" and no "non-calculative" or "essential" thinking of the kind that supposedly gets us beyond beings or things-within-the-world is required to verify such statements as "there are no oranges in the refrigerator" or "there is no money in my pocket" or "Samuel Blau is not suffering from cancer." Absences, if I may talk in this way, are one thing; Heidegger's Nothing, if it is real at all, is quite another. It will be helpful to introduce the terms "natural" and "non-natural" to bring out this distinction. A "natural" fact or phenomenon will be one which can be described in terms of an "empiricist language" as this has been defined by Hempel.[156] A "non-natural" fact or phenomenon, if there is any, could not be described in an empiricist language. Using this terminology, I can state my point by saying that absences are natural phenomena—the absence of oranges or money or cancer *can* be expressed in an empiricist language—while the Nothing is conceded to be a "non-natural" phenomenon or reality.

I next wish to discuss nothingness in the sense of the absence of all things or what I shall call "the total absence." Such a discussion will shed some light on what Heidegger does and what he does not mean by his Nothing. I first wish to show that nothingness in the sense of the absence of all things is a perfectly intelligible notion. I can do this most easily by assuming, for the sake of this discussion, that all things are material and that physics has established a law which I shall call "the principle of continuous reduction of mass-energy." This principle, as the name suggests, asserts that the quantity of mass-energy is constantly diminishing. Let us further suppose that we know the exact amount of mass-energy existing at the present time. We will then be able to predict the ever diminishing quantities existing at later times and we will also be able to predict when the quantity will be zero. At that time nothing would exist; the statement "nothing exists" would have become true; there would be a total absence of things. Of course, the principle of continuous reduction is not a true description of the actual universe and we have no reason whatever to suppose that there ever was or ever will be nothing, i.e., a total absence; but the only point at issue at the moment is that such a state of affairs is logically conceivable.

This conclusion has been challenged by many philosophers. Two of its most prominent opponents in the twentieth century are Bergson and Sartre. Sartre's discussion is exceedingly obscure and I will here consider Bergson's two chief arguments. They are meant to show that the notion of a total absence is a "pseudo-idea, a mere word."[157] Bergson's first argument is based on the consideration that when we think of the non-existence of an object we "replace" it in our thought by another object. It is true that any particular object "can be supposed annihilated." Not realizing that the suppression of a thing consists in the substitution of another, we infer that it is possible to suppress in thought all objects simultaneously and thereby think of a total absence. This inference is fallacious:

> If thinking the absence of one thing is only possible by the more or less explicit representation of the presence of some other thing, if, in short, annihilation signifies before anything else substitution, the idea of an "annihilation of everything" is as absurd as that of a square circle.[158]

Bergson argues in effect that the statement "nothing exists" is not false but self-contradictory because we cannot visualize or, more generally, have an image of a total absence. In reply it should be observed that this argument confuses logical with psychological considerations. It may well be true that we cannot visualize or imagine a total absence, but this shows nothing whatever about the logical status of the statement that nothing exists. From the fact that I or anybody else cannot frame an image of the absence of both of two things, A and B, it does not follow that their simultaneous absence is logically inconceivable, i.e., that the statements "A does not exist" and "B does not exist" cannot be true at the same time. Let us suppose that the universe consists of just three things, A, B, and C. Let us furthermore assume that all human beings are so constituted that whenever they think of the absence of one of these three things, they cannot help thinking of the presence of one of the others. Surely, it would not follow that the simultaneous absence of all three things is logically inconceivable, i.e., that the statements "A does not exist," "B does not exist," and "C does not exist" cannot be true at the same time.

It may be objected that in the above illustration the universe consists not of three, but of at least four objects—A, B, C, and the person thinking about them (we will assume that there is only one such person). The person thinking about A, B, and C, it would be said, has not been "suppressed." This is in effect Bergson's second argument. "From the fact that two relative absences are imaginable in turn," he writes, "we wrongly conclude that they are imaginable together." This conclusion is absurd because we cannot imagine an absence

> without perceiving, at least confusedly, that we are imagining it, consequently that we are acting, that we are thinking, and therefore that something still subsists.[159]

The argument is very similar to one commonly employed to show that we cannot conceive of our own death. It is said that in any attempt to do so we are surreptitiously present as "spectators" of our own annihilation. Bergson himself uses this very illustration to support his case against the conceivability of a total absence:

> I can, no doubt, interrupt by thought the course of my inner life; I may suppose that I sleep without dreaming or that I have ceased to exist; but at the very instant when I make this supposition, I conceive myself, I imagine myself watching over my slumber or surviving my annihilation.[160]

The fallacy of this argument consists in the confusion of the content of a thought with its occurrence in the life of a given person. It is true that I cannot think of anything without being alive, but this shows nothing whatever about the content of my thoughts. More specifically, it does not show that in a given case *what* I am thinking about is one of my thoughts. Let us suppose that on November 11, 1978, I am thinking about the speech which Winston Churchill made to the House of Commons in 1940 after the fall of France. In order to do this I must be alive on November 11, 1978, but *what* I think about is Churchill's speech in 1940 and not my thought about it in 1978. I can think of my own death as easily as of the death of other people. To do this I must be alive, but again what I think about is *my annihilation* and not *my thinking about* my annihilation.[161] Similarly, the fact that I must be alive in order to think about the absence of all things in no way requires me to think about my existence at the time the thought occurs. My existence at that time does indeed show that the statement "nothing exists" is *false*. It does not show, what is the point at issue, that it is self-contradictory or that I am unable to comprehend what *would* make it true.[162]

Is Heidegger's Nothing identical with the total absence just discussed? Heidegger himself has repeatedly disavowed such an identification and, what is more important, his most characteristic pronouncements preclude it. However, he does not have a single consistent position on the subject. Although much of what Heidegger says about anxiety, death and specifically about the Nothing clearly implies that it must be distinguished from the total absence, there are some passages in his earlier writings of which we could not make any sense unless the Nothing is *there* understood as the absence of all things. Thus, at the opening of *An Introduction to Metaphysics* he raises the question, asked before him, among many others, by Leibniz, Voltaire, Schelling and Scheler—"why are there any things at all and not rather Nothing?" He insists that this is a question which no human being can totally avoid, remarking that "each of us is grazed at least once, perhaps more than once, by the hidden power of this question."[163] It must be emphasized, because of what Heidegger wrote in subsequent years, that in the question by whose power each of us has been "grazed," "nothing" means "not anything" so that the whole question comes to "why are there things and not a total absence of things? It should also be observed that although he capitalizes "Nothing" he does not here, as he does on most other occasions, speak of "*the* Nothing." In later retrospective musings Heidegger insists that his question is not identical with the one discussed by Leibniz and Schelling: they were, and he was not, looking for "the highest ground and the first cause of all beings which was itself treated as a being."[164] It is true that Heidegger was not satisfied (and probably not looking for) the kind of answer arrived at by Leibniz and Schelling, but this does not show that he was not asking the same question. In any event he now (1955) tells us that he was really concerned with the question "why do people everywhere give priority to beings and do not rather think about the not of beings, this 'Nothing,' i.e., Being in its essence?" (*Ibid.*) In what was probably Heidegger's last discussion of this issue—in a TV-interview in celebration of his eightieth birthday—he told the interviewer that for him "the question has a totally different sense" from the one it has for Leibniz, Schelling and other metaphysicians. He then explained that *his* question meant "why are beings given priority, why is the Nothing not thought of as identical with Being?" This last question, he goes on, amounts to asking "why is the world dominated by forgetfulness of Being and where does this forgetfulness originate?"[165] Even if one grants that these last questions—about the essence of Being, the identity of Being and the Nothing and the forgetfulness of Being—have some content, it is surely a very strange use of language to ask them by using the words "why are there things and not rather

Nothing?" Moreover, the questions which Heidegger claims to have been concerned with are surely not questions which everybody asks sooner or later and by whose power all of us have been grazed.

There can nevertheless be no doubt that most of the time and certainly in all the passages which are relevant to anxiety and human attitudes in the face of death Heidegger's Nothing is not identical with the total absence. He himself is quite explicit about this in his later writings. In the Postscript to "What Is Metaphysics?" (1943) he writes:

> We are guilty of a "cheap explanation" if we regard the Nothing as "merely negative" ("das bloss Nichtige") and devoid of characteristics.[166]

Again, in a lecture given in 1938 and reprinted in *Holzwege*, he observes that "the Nothing is never nothing just as little as it is something in the sense of being an object."[167] In "Zur Seinsfrage," he explains that the Nothing, just like Being, cannot be said to exist, but is nevertheless real. He tries to convey this by saying that neither Being nor Nothing "ist" ("is"), but that "it gives" both of them. This sounds less peculiar in German since "es gibt" is a common equivalent for "There is."[168] This Nothing "which is not a being . . . is nevertheless nothing negative" and Heidegger angrily defends "What Is Metaphysics?" against the charge of "nihilism" insisting that "the mentioned Nothing is not the Nothing in the sense of the negative Nothing."[169] However, aside from these declarations, there are at least three reasons for not interpreting Heidegger's Nothing as the absence of all things. In the first place, and most obviously, Heidegger believes that " 'it gives' Nothing," i.e., that the Nothing is real *right now* when there are plenty of things. The existence of things implies that the statement "nothing exists" is false in the sense in which it is about the absence of all things; but the existence of things is apparently quite compatible with the reality of Heidegger's Nothing. Secondly, Heidegger's Nothing, as we saw, is a highly active reality. Some passages in *An Introduction to Metaphysics*, in fact, read like a Manichean tract: two deities, a beneficent one called "Being" and a malevolent one called "the Nothing," are battling it out. The former tries to keep things in existence in opposition to the attempts of the latter to destroy them. Again, in Volume 2 of *Nietzsche*, a book composed in the 1930's, he writes: "Being means that beings are and that they are not absent. Being refers to this 'that' as the decisiveness of the insurrection against the Nothing."[170] All such passages about the activities of the Nothing imply that it is not identical with the total absence of things since the latter could not possibly be active. Finally, the total absence can be described in an empiricist language. It is after all just a conjunction of the absence of pears, the absence of money, the absence of elephants, etc. In the imaginary universe governed by the principle of continuous reduction of mass-energy we could predict when the last unit of mass-energy will disappear. The prediction that at a certain time the quantity of mass-energy will be zero would not only be based on just the kind of evidence on which scientific statements are generally founded, but it would also employ only the empirical and logical terms which make up the statements of an empiricist language. Heidegger's Nothing, on the other hand, according to his own declaration, is not the kind of reality which can even in principle be described in an empiricist language.[171]

It is time to return to anxiety and death. I remarked a little earlier that, in his insistence that anxiety (in his special sense) is the mood which corresponds to death, Heidegger calls attention to some interesting facts. I will now try to explain in my own words what these facts are. The fear of death, understood as the fear of *deadness*, is a unique fear. All or at least all the most familiar fears are in one way or another concerned with pain and suffering. We are afraid of "detrimental" objects, to use Heidegger's word, because they are liable to kill us or because they are going to hurt us. We are afraid of objects, but we are also afraid of painful experiences. Deadness, however, is not a painful experience. It is not an experience at all. When I am dead, I will not be in pain, I will not be ill, I will not be rejected, unfairly criticized or in any other way mistreated. However, even after I have realized this, the prospect of deadness continues to be horrifying and at times quite unbearable. In a letter, written not long before his own death, Einstein alluded to the same facts. "Approached rationally," he wrote, "that fear [the fear of death] is the most unjustified of all fears, for there is no risk of any accidents to one who is dead." The fear of death is therefore "stupid," but even so it "cannot be helped."[172]

I am not sure that the words "fear" or "anxiety" or any other term taken from the fear-family are appropriate names for the mood that comes over thoughtful people when they fully realize the finality of death. Whatever the label we decide on, I cannot agree that the mood is "stupid." It is true that when I am dead I will not suffer. It would also be conceded by most people that an infinite period of deadness is greatly preferable to a life of infinite duration which is filled with excruciating pain. At the same time it is difficult to bear the thought that, after I have died, I will be unable—for all eternity—to do any of the things which made life interesting and enjoyable and, what is equally unfortunate, to do any of the things I would have liked to do but never did. The sting here comes from the eternity of the period of nonexistence after death. Death is unlike sleep not only in that is involves the absence of any consciousness, but also in that no return to consciousness is possible. If one were in a state of unconsciousness a few thousand or even a few million years, but if one were assured of a return for, say, another seventy years and if this were followed by further such cycles, the prospect of enormously long periods of total unconsciousness would not be unbearable and might on the contrary be rather pleasing. It is not just the totality of the absence, but the eternity of this totality which most people find so unbearable. From Lucretius on, philosophers have tried to lessen people's concern about death by pointing out that we also did not exist for an infinite period before we were born; and yet we do not feel any similar fear of concern about that non-existence. Unfortunately these reflections do not usually have a soothing effect.

In the absence of any better suggestion I will continue to use Heidegger's word "anxiety" to refer to the mood we have been discussing. We have seen that anxiety in this sense is a mood which *in a sense* does not have an object. I am afraid (or horrified) without being afraid of anything unpleasant that may happen to me, of any painful experiences. I am afraid without being afraid of *any* experiences. This is Heidegger's point and it is a sound observation, but it in no way requires us to subscribe to the reality of his Nothing. A little reflection shows that deadness is another absence. It is true that my deadness, my annihilation, is not an absence I can observe the way I can observe the absence of oranges in the refrigerator or the absence of money in my pocket, but neither could I observe my non-existence before birth. When deadness horrifies me I am concerned about the absence for all eternity of any further experiences that would be *my* experiences, the experiences of Paul Edwards. This absence, like the absence of oranges or the absence of money, can be fully described in the terms of an empiricist language. Using the terminology introduced earlier, it is a "natural" reality. Heidegger's Nothing, on the other hand, by his own stipulation, is a non-natural reality. If we call my non-existence after death, or for that matter my non-existence before birth, "my nothingness," we can say that my nothingness is not Heidegger's Nothing. Even if there is such a reality as his Nothing, it is *not* what we are "face-to-face with" in our anxiety about death.

Summary of Conclusions

It will be helpful to summarize the main conclusions reached in the foregoing discussion, confining ourselves to those which are concerned with Heideggerian assertions about death.

1. Heidegger and Heideggerians assert that all men die isolated and alone. In any of three senses we distinguished, in which "dying alone" means more than "dying," this assertion was found to be false: some people do and some people do not die alone. In effect Heideggerians have redefined "dying alone" so as to make it equivalent to "dying." In this sense the Heideggerian statement is true, but it now simply asserts the platitude that all human beings die.

2. Heidegger and his disciples assert and endlessly repeat that death is untransferable—that nobody can represent, replace or substitute for another in the "matter of dying." In the only straightforward sense of such words as "represent," "replace," and "substitute," this statement is clearly false.

When faced with the facts which show his claim to be false, Heidegger shifts to the two truisms that the death a person dies in his own and that ultimately nobody can prevent another person from dying. The latter of these statements asserts nothing over and above the fact that ultimately everybody dies.

3. Heidegger tells us that human life is "being-towards-death." It is suggested both by Heidegger himself and by numerous other writers that this statement embodies a deep and original insight. When Heidegger's constant conflation of present and future and his confusion of death with concern about death are exposed, it becomes apparent that this doctrine amounts to no more than that, unlike plants and animals, human beings know that they are going to die and that this knowledge influences them in various ways. This is true, but it is a platitude and not a deep and original insight.

4. Heidegger asserts with great emphasis that death is a possibility and not an actuality. In revealing death to be a possibility he is alleged to have "unveiled" its true meaning. Upon analysis, Heidegger's statement that death is a possibility and not an actuality turns out to mean no more than that, after a human being has died, he is an "utter nullity," i.e. that death involves the *total* absence of experiences and behavior. This is nothing other than the view of all the many philosophers and non-philosophers who believe that human beings do not survive death. Any appearance that Heidegger has here made a discovery is due to his outrageous misuse of the word "possibility."

5. The perverse game which Heidegger plays with the word "possibility" has led several of his followers into delivering such bizarre pronouncements as that a person's death is his "capital possibility," or "the crown and culmination" of his life. In this connection we distinguished between dying (which is a succession of states of a living individual) and deadness. To say that deadness is the culmination of a person's life is nonsense. To say that events occurring while a person is dying are the culmination of his life is not nonsense, but if it is asserted as a universal proposition it is certainly false.

6. In the course of supporting his view that death is a possibility Heidegger strenuously opposes any tendency to treat death as a state of some kind. Yet this is precisely what he and his followers do when they engage in the inquiry about the nature of the state in which the dead individual finds himself after he has sustained "the loss of his being." Not surprisingly they find this a baffling question. If we fully realize, as Heidegger evidently has not done, that death is the total absence of experiences and behavior and hence not a state, we see that the question about the nature of the dead person's deadness is a grotesque pseudo-inquiry.

7. Although Heidegger asserts that after death a person is an "utter nullity," he nevertheless also maintains that his philosophy leaves the question of survival entirely open; and many of his followers are ardent believers in life after death. This is a flagrant contradiction and the contradiction is in no way

removed by the manoevre of declaring that "ontologically speaking" death does indeed mean total annihilation, but that "ontically" human beings may nevertheless survive their death.

8. Heidegger distinguishes between fear of dying and anxiety about death. Anxiety brings us face-to-face with "the Nothing." Heidegger makes it clear that this Nothing cannot be described in an empiricist language. Upon examination it is found that although anxiety in this sense is indeed a unique mood in that its object, insofar as it has an object, is not any kind of painful experience but the absence of all experiences, this object cannot be identified with Heidegger's Nothing.

NOTES

1. "Todesdialektik," in *Martin Heidegger zum 70. Geburtstag* (Pfullingen, 1959), p. 94.

2. *What is Existentialism?* (New York, 1964), p. 62. Hereafter cited as *WE*.

3. *Being, Man and Death* (The University of Kentucky, 1970), pp. 2, 5. Hereafter cited as *BMD*. Demske's book is one of two volumes entirely devoted to Heidegger's views of death. The other is Adolf Sternberger's *Der verstandene Tod* (Leipzig, 1934). Sternberger treats Heidegger with respect, but he does offer a few critical comments. Demske's book is pure panegyric. Like the great majority of what passes as Heidegger-commentary, his book largely consists of quotations and paraphrases of Heidegger's remarks, accompanied by ecstatic endorsements.

4. "An English Version of Martin Heidegger's *Being and Time*," *Review of Metaphysics*, 1962, pp. 305, 308. With the possible exception of Herbert Spencer who, in his heyday, was celebrated as "the most capacious and most powerful intellect of all time" compared with whom Aristotle was a "pygmy" and Kant, Hegel, Fichte and Schelling "gropers," there has never been a philosopher who during his lifetime received as much adulation as Heidegger. Karl Rahner, the distinguished Catholic theologian who, as far as I know, is not usually given to such gushy effusions, in a talk on German television first observes—what seems to me highly questionable—that "contemporary Catholic theology is unthinkable without Martin Heidegger." He then gratefully acknowledges that Heidegger has "taught us to be able to look in anything and everything for that *ineffable secret* which *disposes* ("verfügt") over us." Finally, he addresses Heidegger as his "master" and "simply and modestly confesses" that although he had many good "schoolmasters," he had only "*one* whom he could revere as his *teacher*." (R. Wisser, ed., *Martin Heidegger im Gespräch*, [Freiburg and Munich, 1970], pp. 48–49, Rahner's italics throughout). For Werner Marx, professor of philosophy at Freiburg and one of the leading Heidegger-scholars in the world, Heidegger is much more than a great teacher. "As Kierkegaard leaped from the religious stage toward an awareness of the 'wholly other'," he writes, so Heidegger leaps "onto the shores of Being." After the leap Heidegger became "imbued with a strong conviction," shared by Marx, that "he is the voice and instrument of Being." In his capacity as the hierophant of Being he is trying to "attain a 'second beginning' for

mankind." ("Heidegger's New Conception of Philosophy—The Second Phase of 'Existentialism'," *Social Research*, Winter, 1955, pp. 474, 467). I have often wondered in connection with such claims what the first beginning is supposed to have been. As a third illustration I will quote the later Hannah Arendt. She concludes an article on "Martin Heidegger at Eighty," published in the *New York Review* of October 21, 1971, with the following, quite uncharacteristic, lyrical outburst: "the wind that blows through Heidegger's thinking—like that which still sweeps toward us after thousands of years from the work of Plato—does not spring from the century he happens to live in. It comes from the primeval, and what it leaves behind is something perfect, something which, like everything perfect (in Rilke's words), falls back to where it came from." I will refrain from commenting on this primeval wind and its strange deposit. However, having mentioned Arendt's article, I cannot in good conscience refrain from calling attention to the utterly disgraceful coverup it contains of Heidegger's well-documented activities during the Nazi period. Most American and British readers are not aware that, aside from his ardent public support of the Nazi dictatorship for several years, Heidegger engaged in such acts as deleting the dedication to his teacher and benefactor, Edmund Husserl (who was a Jew), from the fifth edition of *Being and Time*. There is every reason to suppose that if Heidegger had shown the slightest firmness (and decency) the dedication need not have been eliminated. Wilhelm Furtwängler, who, unlike Heidegger, was not a member of the Nazi party, repeatedly opposed anti-Semitic directives issued by Nazi officials and he usually got his way. Anybody who reads Hannah Arendt's double-talk, or the double-talk of other Heideggerian apologists, should take the trouble to check it against the documents compiled by Guido Schneeberger in *Nachlese zu Heidegger* (Bern, 1962). My final illustration comes from the 14th edition of Heinrich Schmidt's *Philosophisches Wörterbuch*, edited by Georgi Schischkoff, (Stuttgart, 1957), a reference work which aspires to be both authoritative and impartial. The article on Heidegger (which is twice as long as the article on Hume and eight times as long as the one on Wittgenstein) concludes with the following ovation: "Every philosopher and indeed every poet and writer who has anything to say to the world must come to terms with Heidegger, consciously or else unconsciously. His philosophy opens a new era in the histroy of European thought." (p. 233) In spite of strong temptation I have abstained throughout this monograph from any discussion of the psychology of Heidegger-worship which must surely be one of the strangest aberrations in the intellectual history of our times.

5. *Being and Time*, English translation by John Macquarrie and Edward Robinson (London, 1962), p. 308. My quotations are for the most part from this translation, hereafter cited as M-R. Although M-R is in many ways an admirable job, on some occasions the translators, in trying to be idiomatic and avoid excessive literalness, do not give the reader an adequate idea of Heidegger's evident intentions. In such cases I have provided my own translation. Whenever I depart, to any extent, from M-R I give page references to the original German text prefaced by "G" as well as to the corresponding page in M-R. *Being and Time*. Hereafter cited as *BT*.

6. *BT*, p. 308. Heidegger's original is "einzig von ihm selbst her . . . übernehmen" which means "taken over by [Dasein] itself exclusively." The M-R translation is idiomatically quite correct in using "alone."

7. *An Existentialist Theology* (London, 1955), p. 118. Hereafter cited as *ET*.

8. *The Challenge of Existentialism* (Bloomington, 1959), p. 82. Hereafter cited as *CE*.

9. *Ibid.*, p. 108.

10. *Existence and Freedom* (Evanston, 1961), p. 108. Hereafter cited as *EF*.

11. *BMD*, p. 32.

12. *The Moment of Truth* (London, 1965), p. 1. Hereafter cited as *MT*.

13. *A Commentary on Heidegger's "Being and Time"* (New York, 1970), pp. 150–51. Hereafter cited as *CBT*.

14. "The Problem of Death in Modern Philosophy," in N. A. Scott Jr. (ed.), *The Modern Vision of Death*, (Richmond, Virginia, 1967), p. 55. Hereafter cited as PD.

15. *Ibid.*, p. 56.

16. *Heidegger—Through Phenomenology to Thought*, 2d ed., with a Preface by Heidegger, (The Hague, 1967), p. 76.

17. *Heidegger* (London, 1957), p. 45.

18. *New York Times*, Dec. 9, 1973.

19. "My Own Life," reprinted in Norman Kemp Smith (ed.), *Hume's Dialogues Concerning Natural Religion* (Edinburgh, 1935), p. 239. The same volume contains the letter from Adam Smith to William Strahan describing Hume's last months. Both these documents are also reprinted in J. Y. T. Greig (ed.), *The Letters of David Hume*, Vol. II (Oxford, 1932). The last-mentioned book contains the remarkable letter from Hume to Edward Gibbon upon reading the first volume of *The Decline and Fall of the Roman Empire*, which appeared while Hume was dying.

20. *The Savage God* (London and New York, 1971), p. 190.

21. Vaché was twenty-three when he killed himself. There is much interesting information about him in Hans Richter, *Dadá* (London and New York, 1965), on which Alvarez's account is based, and in Maurice Nadau, *The History of Surrealism* (London, 1968).

22. For a detailed discussion of this notion, implicit in many of our ordinary sayings about death, *see* the first section of my article "Existentialism and Death: A Survey of some Confusions and Absurdities," in S. Morgenbesser, *et al.*, *Philosophy, Science and Method—Essays in Honor of Ernest Nagel* (New York, 1969). Hereafter cited as ED.

23. *BMD*, p. 37.

24. PD, p. 56.

25. *Ibid.*, p. 62.

26. The German original is "Tod *ist* je nur eigener." M-R mistranslate this as "Death is just one's own." The word "je" which is short for "jeweils" means "always" and not "just."

27. *Die Philosophie der Existenz* (Vienna, 1952), pp. 258–59. Although Knittermeyer greatly admires both Jaspers and Sartre, he insists that neither of them can be compared with Heidegger as regards "originality of thinking or formulation." (p. 207)

28. *Existenzphilosophie*, 2d ed., (Hamburg, 1949), p. 26.

29. This passage is quoted from p. 228 of the complete Indian edition of 1967, published in Varanasi by Banaras Hindu University Press. The remark about Mehta's meetings with Heidegger is taken from p. xix of the Preface to the abbreviated American edition (New York: Harper & Row, 1971). The praise of Mehta comes from the *Review of Metaphysics*, 1973, pp. 760–61. It is by Jack D. Caputo.

30. *CE*, p. 239.

31. PD, pp. 54–55.

32. *EF*, p. 114.

33. *CBT*, pp. 150 and 142.

34. "Three Directions of Phenomenology," in M. Grene (ed.), *The Anatomy of Knowledge* (Amherst, 1969), p. 270. In fairness it should be added that, although Bossart treats Heidegger with great respect, unlike the other writers quoted here, he does not appear to be an uncritical admirer.

35. "The Listener," February 16, 1978, p. 202.

36. *EF*, p. 100.
37. *Ibid.*, p. 113.
38. *Ibid.*, pp. 102–03.
39. *Ibid.*, p. 102, my italics.
40. *Ibid.*, p. 103.
41. *Ibid.*, p. 113, my italics.
42. "The Listener," *op. cit.*
43. *WE*, p. 63.
44. *EF*, p. 98.
45. *Ibid.*, p. 96.
46. *Ibid.*, p. 95, Schrag's italics.
47. *BMD*, p. 72, my italics.
48. *Ibid.*, p. 7.
49. *Ibid.*, p. 25, Demske's italics.
50. PD, p. 53.
51. *Ibid.*, p. 8, Boros's italics.
52. "The Listener," *op. cit.*
53. *WE*, p. 63, my italics.
54. *EF*, p. 112.
55. *Ibid.*, p. 112.
56. *Ibid.*
57. *Ibid.*, p. 113.
58. *Ibid.*, p. 108.
59. *Ibid.*, p. 97.
60. *CBT*, p. 147.
61. *EF*, p. 127.
62. *Ibid.*, p. 141.
63. *Ibid.*, p. 146, Schrag's italics.
64. PD, pp. 59–60.
65. In addition to distinguishing between biological death and death in the "existential" sense which is being-towards-death, Heidegger distinguishes two different senses of biological death. The former of these he calls "Verenden" and the latter "Ableben" which M-R translate as "perish" and "demise" respectively. Plants and animals "perish." Dasein never perishes. It "demises." (p. 291) "Ableben" or "demising," according to Schrag, "refers to the biological termination of human life or man's ontic annihilation." I assume that the distinction between "perishing" and "demising" is meant to do justice to the fact that human beings are in a sense more than biological organisms, that they are conscious beings and that their death involves the end of their mental and not only of their physical existence. I am not sure that this is what is meant because the higher animals, too, are conscious beings and also because talking in this way implies a dualism to which Heidegger seems to be opposed elsewhere in *BT*. Without denying the various differences between human beings on the one hand and plants and animals on the other, I do not see that we have here two different senses of biological "death" or two different senses of "ending." I shall say more about this last topic at the end of the present section.
66. *BMD*, p. 95.
67. It is amazing that Barrett's interviewer, Bryan Magee, did not offer a single demurrer. On the contrary, he was greatly impressed and told the audience that he had found Heidegger's teaching (as expounded by Barrett) "deeply congenial." Later in the interview Barrett declared that, unlike Sartre, Heidegger "is really saturated with a sense of being." I trust that some day either Magee or Barrett will explain what it is

to be "saturated with a sense of being." The entire interview was a scandalous lapse from the BBC's customary high standards in the treatment of philosophical issues.

68. *BMD.*, p. 200.

69. *Ibid.* It should be pointed out in fairness to Tanabe, that his article is not at all concerned with Demske's question. His statements that man "lives dying" and "dies living" are incidental to his larger themes. These include the grounding of all that is temporal and finite in the Infinite-Absolute which is also the Eternal, the nature of the "absolute Nothing" and the "concrete origin" of Heidegger's "Ereignis" ("The Event"). Tanabe offers numerous highly illuminating remarks which should be of special interest to students of the Nothing. In connection with the "concrete origin" of Heidegger's "Ereignis" Tanabe tells us that "dialectic turns back into the Nothing as the self-negation of Being and thereby denies the identity of thinking and Being in the mode of total negation, i.e., as neither identical nor non-identical." (p. 126) A few pages later we are presented with the following pearl: "The Absolute Nothing or the Nothing of the Nothing loves and essentially affirms all that is real." (p. 129) Philosophers who have been puzzled about the nature of freedom will be interested in Tanabe's views on the subject: "Free choice occurs in the Nothing as a crack and [as] an empty gaping hole of the self-negation of the eternal which has been disrupted in repetition." (p. 103) Father Demske deserves special credit for rescuing this remarkable essay from oblivion.

70. It is equally necessary for the "solution" of Heidegger's "wholeness" problem which I have had to neglect in this study. I should add that not all of Heidegger's notions about time are absurd. He has one interesting point which he himself states with extreme obscurity but which has recently been restated in more accessible language by C. M. Sherover in *Heidegger, Kant and Time* (Bloomington, 1971, *see* especially pp. 191ff and 260ff).

71. *Being and Death* (Berkeley and Los Angeles, 1965), p. 117.

72. *Existential Phenomenology*, revised edition, (Pittsburgh, 1969), p. 393.

73. *Martin Heidegger* (Richmond, 1968), p. 62.

74. *ET*, p. 119.

75. *BMT*, p. 20.

76. "Ausgezeichnet" is a perfectly common German word meaning "splendid," "excellent," "outstanding," "distinguished," "first-class." When I went to high school in Vienna, the highest grade for a course, corresponding to the "A" of American schools, was "ausgezeichnet." It is used only as a term of praise; and if Heidegger meant anything less than "splendid" or "excellent possibility," he certainly picked a most unfortunate word. Even if, in fact, he means nothing more than what is meant by the English "distinctive" (which itself is far from clear in this context), the word "ausgezeichnet" will continue to have the old associations for most readers.

77. PD, pp. 54, 61.

78. *Op. cit.*, pp. 390–91. Luijpen also characterizes death as the "highest instance" (whatever this means) of man's being-in-the-world (p. 398).

79. *Studies in Christian Existentialism* (London, 1966), p. 55. Hereafter cited as *SCE*.

80. *BMD*, p. 25.

81. *In Sachen Heidegger* (Munich, 1961), p. 78. In the passage from which I quote Hühnerfeld states and endorses what he takes to be Heidegger's message. It should be added that Hühnerfeld's book is not another string of paraphrases and panegyrics masquerading as a commentary on Heidegger's philosophy. On the contrary, it is a book of much interest containing more biographical material about Heidegger than any other source I know. Hühnerfeld did not at all admire Heidegger's character and

he regarded his influence as in many ways unwholesome. This critical judgment did not, however, extend to Heidegger's philosophy. It is regrettable that, as the result of a car accident, Hühnerfeld attained the "crown" of his life at the early age of thirty-four.

82. *EF*, p. 108.

83. *Ibid*.

84. *CE*, p. 83, my italics.

85. Macquarrie is the only Heideggerian who shows any awareness that Heidegger is using the word "possibility" in a strange way here. He admits (*SCE*, p. 54) that it is "very odd to talk of death as a possibility at all" and, like Heidegger, he finds it necessary to explain that Heidegger is not asking us to "rush suicidally into death." (*Ibid*.) However, Macquarrie shows not the slightest awareness that there has been a shift in Heidegger's use of "possibility" and that the word in this context does not mean what it had meant throughout *BT*. Gelven discusses at some length what he calls Heidegger's "principle that possibility is prior to actuality." This principle, he tells us, is "rampant in Heidegger's thought," (*op. cit*., p. 75) but it does not once occur to him that when Heidegger contrasts possibility with actuality in connection with death, we are no longer presented with the principle that had been "rampant" in the earlier chapters.

86. Gelven is much impressed by this feature of Heidegger's presentation. "His style," Gelven observes, "is almost that of the mystery-story writer—by making the mystery seem so insoluble, the success of the brilliant detective is all the more admired." Gelven adds that "this is a legitimate part of Heidegger's charm as a great teacher." (*op. cit*., p. 146) Gelven's book consists mostly of repetitions of Heideggerian formulations in the obscure language of the original, followed by little cries of love such as "brilliant," "acute," and "even more acute." I am indebted to him for the discovery that "in spite of its rather frequent occurrence death comes only once for each person." (142)

87. *Why I Am Not a Christian*, (New York, 1957), p. 54.

88. For a fuller discussion of this point *see* my article ED, *op. cit*., pp. 482ff.

89. *Op. cit*., p. 155. Although "translations cannot carry the full subtlety of the meaning," it is reassuring to know that one need not be a "native German" to be receptive to this enlightenment.

90. *EF*, p. 115.

91. *Ibid*., p. 113.

92. *Being and Nothingness*, (New York, 1956), p. 537, Sartre's italics.

93. *MT*, p. 1

94. *Ibid*., my italics.

95. *SCE*, p. 57.

96. *Ibid*., p. 51, Macquarrie's italics.

97. *Ibid*.

98. *ET*, p. 117.

99. *SCE*, p. 52; *ET*, p. 117.

100. *SCE*, p. 52, my italics.

101. *ET*, p. 118.

102. J. Ferrater Mora is another philosopher who is seriously concerned to explore the inner nature of the death of the deceased. In *Being and Death* (*op. cit*., pp. 175 —76) he states the predicament of anybody engaging in such an investigation: "We can 'see' that people die; we can think of our own death as an event which will take place sooner or later, but we do not seem to be able to experience death in the same way as we do other 'events' such as pleasure, pain, good health, illness, senility. All we can

'see' of death is its 'residue,' for example, a corpse . . ." It should be noted that a dead person is here automatically regarded as more than a corpse. For a detailed critique of the grotesque confusions in Mora's answer to this problem—especially the notion that a survivor can "share" the dead person's death—*see* my article ED, *op. cit.*, pp. 480–81 and 487–91.

103. *MT*, p. 8.

104. *SCE*, p. 51.

105. *Ibid.*, p. 55.

106. In *Der Feldweg* (a little essay published in 1953) Heidegger writes that "knowing joy is a door to the eternal." (Frankfurt, 1953), p. 6. We are not told whether this is to be construed as an "ontic" decision in favor of survival.

107. *EF*, p. 117.

108. *Ibid.*, p. 118.

109. "Grundzüge Heideggerschen Philosophierens," *Zeitschrift für Philosophische Forschung*, 1950–51, p. 562.

110. *Ibid.*, p. 118.

111. *Ibid.*, p. 110.

112. *The Phenomenological Movement*, vol. II, 2d ed. (The Hague, 1965), p. 290.

113. "The Aristotelian Versus the Heideggerian Approach to the Problem of Technology," in C. Mitcham and R. Mackey (eds.), *Philosophy and Technology*, (New York, 1972), p. 253.

114. *BMD*, p. 17.

115. *Irrational Man*, (New York, 1958), p. 210.

116. *Vom Wesen der Wahrheit*, (Frankfurt, 1943), pp. 19, 23 and 25. In this monograph I have tried to keep away from Heidegger's so-called "quest" for Being. So far as I can see, Heidegger and Heideggerians are primarily concerned to advocate two doctrines in this connection (without realizing that they are distinct)—(1) that Being or "Beingness" or "isness" (as they frequently call it) is the basic common characteristic of all beings and (2) that it is the mysterious "ground," "source," or "warranter" of beings. It can be shown, I think, that the first of these doctrines is false and that the second is incoherent. Heidegger's quest for Being is the topic to which I am devoting most attention in my book on Heidegger mentioned in the Preface.

117. *Martin Heidegger on Being Human*, (New York, 1969), p. 17.

118. For a detailed discussion of the confusion between genetic and logical questions on the part of religious existentialists *see* my Lindley Lecture, *Buber and Buberism—A Critical Evaluation* (Lawrence, Kansas: The University of Kansas Press, 1970), pp. 44f.

119. "The Vitality of Death," *The Journal of Existentialism*, 1964, p. 156.

120. *Ibid.*, p. 158.

121. *Philosophy: A General Introduction* (New York, 1968), pp. 305–06.

122. *Ibid.*, p. 313.

123. *Managing Anxiety* (Englewood-Cliffs, 1974), p. 173.

124. *Ibid.*, p. 176.

125. *Ibid.*, p. 126.

126. (Englewood-Cliffs, 1976), pp. 188ff. Besides assurance of indestructibility, Koestenbaum's "Immortality Exercises" are supposed to provide vast psychological benefits: "Your life can now be lived with simple grace. Gone is the hurry, the anguish, the despair, the panic; there is no further need to protect yourself against anxiety. Gone will be compulsive behavior and obsessive ideas." (p. 196) Koestenbaum's fertile imagination is nowhere more evident than in his treatment of Bertrand Russell's theory of types which he appears to hold responsible for most of the ills of

the world, or, at any rate, for the sterility and degradation of contemporary philosophy and psychology. Because Russell "artificially distorts language to avoid self-reference, he makes it illicit to explore subjectivity. . . . Thus, the only proper task for philosophy becomes the study of objects, which is usually called the scientific enterprise. The study of man—i.e., the study of the nature of consciousness and of subjectivity—originally the primary task of philosophic inspiration—is now to be abandoned altogether." We are then offered what I can only call a startling "summary" of Russell's theory: "In sum, what Russell is really saying is that we must not philosophize about the child with separation anxiety." (p. 170) Against "such dangerous and nefarious dèhumanization," Koestenbaum, as spokesman for the "existential-phenomenological exploration of subjectivity," is obliged to "take a firm stand". (*Ibid.*) I have a feeling that Russell's reputation will survive this devastating judgment. Koestenbaum's farrago of impudent and shoddy fantasies is hailed by Dr. Kübler-Ross as "an enormous piece of work" and by Dr. Viktor Frankl as "a sound philosophy." The book is published in a series whose general editors are the existential psychologist Charles Hampden-Turner and Rollo May. One cannot help wondering what Hampden-Turner, May, Kübler-Ross or Frankl know about the theory of types.

127. PD, pp. 55–56.

128. *Ibid.*

129. *Ibid.*, p. 62.

130. *Ibid.*, p. 67.

131. *SCE.*

132. Lest the remarks in the text be misunderstood, I hasten to add that many Catholic and Protestant philosophers are anything but supporters of Heidegger's ideas. Anthony Kenny, an Oxford philosopher of great ability who is also a Catholic, has repeatedly expressed his contempt both for Heidegger himself and for various of his followers. Thus, in a review of Paul Ricoeur's contribution to a book entitled *The Religious Significance of Atheism*, Kenny writes: "Ricoeur's discussion is shored up, at crucial points, by gaseous quotations from Heidegger in which the obvious is reiterated with bombinating opacity." ("The Listener," February 5, 1970). Father Copleston, whose standing as a philosopher and as a historian of philosophy compares more than favorably with that of such Heideggerian clerics as Fathers Richardson, Demske, and Boros, treats Heidegger with disdain in Vol. 7 of his monumental *History of Philosphy* (London, 1963), pp. 437f.

133. I am following M-R in using "anxiety" for "Angst" and "fear" for "Furcht." The translators of "What Is Metaphysics?" in *Existence and Being* (an exceedingly shoddy and inaccurate translation) render "Angst" as "dread." M-R reserve "dread" for the species of fear to which Heidegger refers as "Grauen." (p. 182; G. 142)

134. *Main Currents in Contemporary German, British, and American Philosophy*, tr. A. D. Blumberg, (Dordrecht-Holland, 1969), p. 179.

135. *Op. cit.*, p. 161.

136. *Concluding Unscientific Postscript*, tr. D. F. Swenson (Princeton, 1941), pp. 182ff.

137. "Was ist Metaphysik?" reprinted in Heidegger's *Wegmarken* (Frankfurt, 1967), pp. 8–9. Hereafter cited as *W*. All quotations from "Was ist Metaphysik?" are given in my own translation.

138. It is clearly Heidegger's view that when we think about death authentically we experience anxiety. It is not clear whether he is committed to the converse—to the view that anxiety is always anxiety of death ("Todesangst"). This is not clear because of the obscurity of his various remarks that the "wovor" of anxiety is "the world as such" and "being-in-the-world-itself." None of this is ever adequately explained,

either by Heidegger or by any of his devotees. Otto Pöggeler, a leading Heidegger-scholar, does not seem to be sure either. In one passage (*Der Denkweg Martin Heideggers*, [Pfullingen, 1963], p. 301) he speaks of "anxiety which is *essentially* anxiety of death," (my italics) leaving open the possibility that anxiety can also be experienced in situations in which we are not face to face with death.

139. *Einführung in die Metaphysik* 2d ed., (Tübingen: Niemeyer, 1958), pp. 19–20. An English translation of this book by Ralph Manheim was published by Yale University Press in 1959. Manheim's translation is a respectable job, but seriously misleads the reader in translating Heidegger's "das Nichts" simply as "nothing" without even capitalizing the word. English translations of Heidegger's books do not usually receive critical reviews by analytic philosophers. This volume is an exception. It was reviewed incisively and amusingly both by Walter Cerf in *Philosophy and Phenomenological Research*, 1961, pp. 109–112 and by Anthony Quinton in *Philosophical Books*, 1960, pp. 11–13.

140. *W*, p. 18.

141. *W*, pp. 17–18. The German original is: "dieses wissenschaftliche Dasein ist nur möglich, wenn es sich im vorhinein in das Nichts hineinhält."

142. Pfullingen, 1961, p. 51.

143. The word "datum" is not Heidegger's, but that of his follower, William Barrett (*Irrational Man, op. cit.*, p. 252). Barrett also refers to the Nothing as "a strange negative entity." (*Ibid.*) Heidegger himself would probably wish to avoid the word "entity," but he would approve of the remainder of this description. The Nothing, as we found, is inaccessible to science or ordinary observation quite unlike "the rain outside or the mountain or any object whatsoever." Arne Naess, in an exceedingly sympathetic presentation, speaks of the Nothing as a "phenomenon." "Insofar as the nothing is disclosed," writes Naess, "it is a 'phenomenon' in the first of the senses of the word Heidegger has announced he will use in his text. In this sense a phenomenon is something which shows-itself-by-itself." (*Four Modern Philosphers*, [Chicago, 1968], p. 225).

144. *W*, p. 14.

145. *Ibid.*, pp. 5–6.

146. *Ibid.*

147. *Ibid.*, pp. 13–14.

148. *Ibid.*, p. 14.

149. *My Search for Absolutes*, (New York, 1967), pp. 81–82.

150. *SCE*, p. 85.

151. *Ibid.*, p. 83.

152. *Ibid.*, p. 85.

153. *Ibid.*, p. 82.

154. *The Monist*, 1918–1919, reprinted in Russell's *Logic and Knowledge* (London, 1956).

155. Readers interested in these questions will find informative and clarifying discussions in A. N. Prior's articles "Negation" and "Correspondence Theory of Truth" (*Encyclopedia of Philosophy*, Vol. 5, pp. 458–63 and Vol. 2, pp. 223–32) and in the writings of Frank Ramsey, the later Wittgenstein and the later G. E. Moore on which Prior's discussions are based. The dispute over the "existence" of negative facts does involve the entirely intelligible question whether, in Prior's words, "signs of negation are really indispensable—whether what we say when we use them cannot be also said without them, and that more directly—whether signs of negation are just convenient abbreviations for complex forms in which no such signs enter." It should be emphasized that whatever the answer to this question turns out to be, it cannot affect what I

pointed out in the text, namely, that there are true statements containing signs of negation. These statements will remain true even if it should turn out that they are translatable into statements containing no signs of negation.

156. *See* his article "The Empiricist Criterion of Meaning," Section 3. This article is available in many places, most conveniently in A. J. Ayer (ed.), *Logical Positivism* (New York, 1959).

157. *Creative Evolution*, tr. A. Mitchell (New York, 1911), p. 308. All quotations in the text are from the Modern Library reprint of 1944. Sidney Hook, in his "The Quest for 'Being'," wholeheartedly endorses Bergson's "striking analysis" and makes it the basis of an argument against Heidegger's Nothing (*Journal of Philosophy*, 1953, pp. 711ff). For an illuminating critical discussion of Sartre's various pronouncements about nothingness, *see* A. Plantinga, "An Existentialist's Ethics," *The Review of Metaphysics*, 1958.

158. *Ibid.*

159. *Ibid.*, p. 303. I have substituted "absence" for the quaint word "nought" used by Bergson's translator. The French word is "le néant."

160. *Ibid.*, p. 307. Bergson's argument is quite similar to one employed by Berkeley to prove that the notion of unperceived objects is self-contradictory (*The Principles of Human Knowledge*, Section 23): "But say you, surely there is nothing easier than to imagine trees, for instance, in a park, or books existing in a closet, and nobody to perceive them. I answer, you may so, there is no difficulty in it: but what is all this, I beseech you, more than framing in your mind certain ideas which you call *books* and *trees*, and at the same time omitting to frame the idea of any one that may perceive them? *but do not you yourself perceive or think of them all the while?*" (Berkeley's italics). The answer to Berkeley is exactly the same as the one to Bergson given in the text.

161. For a detailed discussion of the confusions of philosophers and others who believe that one's own death is inconceivable, *see* my article " 'My Death'," *Encyclopedia of Philosophy* (New York, 1967), Vol. 5, pp. 416ff.

162. The remarks in the text are sufficient to answer Bergson, but they require one significant qualification. The logical status of "nothing exists now" is different in one interesting respect from that of the statements "nothing will exist in the future" and "nothing existed at some time in the past." The latter two statements are not necessarily false, but the statement "nothing exists now," uttered while the author of the statement exists, although not self-contradictory, is in a sense necessarily false. In this respect it is analogous to the statement "I do not exist." Both are instances of what, I believe, some writers have called "pragmatic contradictions." I am grateful to Mr. Levy for calling my attention to this point.

163. *Op. cit.*, p. 1.

164. "Zur Seinsfrage," *W*, p. 248.

165. *Martin Heidegger im Gespräch, op. cit.*, p. 75.

166. *W*, p. 102.

167. *Holzwege* (Frankfurt, 1950), p. 104.

168. In most of his later writings, when Heidegger wishes to speak of the kind of reality possessed by Being, the Nothing or "the Fourfold" (a curious notion that occupies a central role in his writings after 1950 with which we are not concerned) he uses "wesen," a verb he coined specially for this purpose. Sentences like "Das Sein west" or "das Nichts west" are common throughout Heidegger's later works. There is a German noun "Wesen" which means "essence," but Heidegger derives his verb from the German word "Anwesenheit" which means presence. Heidegger repeatedly speaks of the "Anwesenheit des anwesenden" ("The presence of the Present"). Some

of his more unrestrained American disciples have followed Heidegger's example and coined the verb "to presence." Their translations of Heidegger as well as their own writings abound with the sentence "the Presence presences." Heidegger attributes the insight that "the Presence presences" to the pre-Socratics. He merely claims to have rediscovered it. Unfortunately explanations of what this pronouncement means are not provided. Both here and elsewhere Heidegger and his followers appear to operate on the principle that, if it is repeated often enough, even the most nebulous locution will become familiar and *seem* to be intelligible. It is well to recall a comment made by Cardinal Newman: "Nothing is more common than for men to think that because they are familiar with words, they understand the ideas they stand for."

169. *W*, p. 247.

170. *Op. cit.*, p. 399.

171. I believe that this account fairly reproduces the dominant trend in Heidegger's views about the Nothing. However, for the sake of completeness, it must be mentioned that in his later writings, as some passages quoted earlier indicated, he frequently identified the Nothing with Being. Thus, in the passage in *Holzwege* which I quoted in the text and in which Heidegger assures us that "the Nothing is never nothing," he proceeds to assert that it "is Being itself." Similarly, in the Preface to the third edition of *Vom Wesen des Grundes* (1949) he writes: "The Nothing is the Not of beings and thus is Being experienced from the point of view of beings." (*W*, p. 21) In the Postscript to "What Is Metaphysics?" he is equally definite: "The Nothing . . . unveils itself as that which is distinct from all beings, to which we refer as 'Being'." (*W*, p. 106) Finally, in "Zur Seinsfrage," in his retrospective discussion of what he supposedly did in "What Is Metaphysics?" Heidegger tells us that "since the question 'what is metaphysics?' thinks right from the start only . . . the transcendens, the Being of beings, it can reach the Not of beings, *that* Nothing which is . . . identical with Being." (*W*, p. 249) Heidegger evidently identifies the Nothing with Being on the ground that both are "other than" or distinct from beings. This is a highly dubious reason, for even if one grants that there are realities which transcend beings, it is not at all obvious that they must all be one and the same. The identification of the Nothing with Being is also completely inconsistent with all the Manichean passages found in the writings of the 1930s which seem to express an essential feature of Heidegger's "ontology."

172. Quoted by Banesch Hoffman in *Albert Einstein, Creator and Rebel* (New York, 1972), p. 261.

Printed in the USA
CPSIA information can be obtained
at www.ICGtesting.com
JSHW082222140824
68134JS00015B/680